Discovering
Meditation

*How to practise meditation
techniques to find inner calm
and resolution*

DIANA BRUETON

How To Books

With deep gratitude to Osho,
whose teachings were my way into meditation

First published in 1999 by
How To Books Ltd, 3 Newtec Place,
Magdalen Road, Oxford OX4 1RE, United Kingdom
Tel: (01865) 793806   Fax: (01865) 248780
email: info@howtobooks.co.uk
http://www.howtobooks.co.uk

British Library Cataloguing in Publication Data
A catalogue record for this book is available from
the British Library

Cartoons by Mike Flanagan
Editing by Barbara Massam
Cover design by Shireen Nathoo Design
Cover image PhotoDisc

Produced for How To Books by Deer Park Productions
Typeset by Euroset, Alresford, Hampshire SO24 9PQ
Printed and bound by Cromwell Press, Trowbridge, Wiltshire

NOTE: The material contained in this book is set out in good
faith for general guidance and no liability can be accepted
for loss or expense incurred as a result of relying in particular
circumstances on statements made in the book. The laws
and regulations are complex and liable to change, and readers
should check the current position with the relevant authorities
before making personal arrangements.

Contents

List of illustrations   8

Preface   9

1 Understanding what meditation is   **11**
Looking at meditation   11
Seeing what happens in meditation   12
Deciding you want to meditate   14
Knowing the benefits of meditation   16
Examining the evidence for improved health   16
Questions and answers   21
Summary   21

2 Establishing a basic meditation   **22**
Beginning simply   22
Stilling yourself   23
Meditating on the breath – the basic meditation   25
Adding to the basic technique   28
Quietening the mind   29
Questions and answers   29
Summary   30

3 Setting up a regular practice   **32**
Making a decision to meditate   32
Establishing a practice   33
Choosing when, where and how   35
Finding the right time   36
Setting up a meditation space   36
Having a particular meditation place   37
Getting practical about your routine   38
Questions and answers   41
Summary   42

4   Using traditional meditations   **43**
       Witnessing your thoughts and feelings   43
       Exploring traditional breathing meditations   44
       Trying other traditional meditations   45
       Questions and answers   49
       Summary   50

5   Trying more meditations   **51**
       Gazing meditations   51
       Looking at transcendental meditation   54
       Using sound   54
       Trying more techniques   57
       Working with the chakras   58
       Questions and answers   61

6   Meditating to reduce stress   **62**
       Softening and relaxing   62
       Releasing stress through meditation   63
       Letting go of anxiety   67
       Cultivating inner calm   68
       Using meditation to help rest and sleep   71
       Questions and answers   74
       Summary   74

7   Using active meditations   **75**
       Raising your energy levels   75
       Moving into stillness   77
       Combining inner stillness with outer activity   79
       Bringing meditation into everyday life   80
       Exploring creativity through meditation   83
       Questions and answers   84
       Summary   84

8   Relaxing and meditating   **85**
       Comparing meditation and relaxation   85
       Relaxing before a meditation   86
       Progressive relaxation   86
       Using relaxation techniques   87
       Questions and answers   89
       Summary   89

9   Using other techniques to help meditation   90
Looking at guided visualisation   90
Trying some guided visualisations   91
Releasing anxiety through visualisation   96
Developing your own visualisations   96
Using other self-help methods   97
Questions and answers   99
Summary   99

10   Meditating with others   100
Joining a meditation group   100
Meditating as a group   101
Meditating with a friend or partner   102
Meditating with children   102
Going on a meditation retreat   103
Going abroad   104
Meditating in a religious context   105
Questions and answers   106
Summary   107

Glossary   108

Useful addresses   110

Further reading   114

Index   116

List of Illustrations

1   Checklist for meditating   15
2   The physical effects of meditation and relaxation techniques   19
3   Making a tape for the basic breath meditation   24
4   Sitting positions for meditation   40
5   A mandala for meditation   53
6   The chakra system   59

Preface

What would you say if someone offered you a way to improve your health, relieve stress, become happier, have more self-esteem and better relationships? You might ask what the catch was, and almost certainly how much it would cost you. If you heard it cost nothing and only required you to sit quietly for about 15–20 minutes twice a day, you might still be sceptical.

Perhaps the fact that meditation has been practised for thousands of years, and that science can now prove that it improves mental, emotional and physical health, would reassure you. But meditation has so much more to offer than improved health.

A seriously ill woman once said to me, 'You know, since the diagnosis everything has become so much more *intense*. I don't mean just my feelings – I mean I notice the flowers and they seem so much more colourful, I'm amazed at what a cup of tea really tastes like, everything is just so much more *real*.' I felt this woman's insight had a really important message for most of us. It's not possible to always maintain that degree of intensity – we need times of 'daydreaming' too – but if we can cultivate even a small degree of this woman's aliveness to her self and her surroundings, hopefully without having to get ill, we would be richer in all aspects of our lives. Meditation *is* a way of coming more alive in every way.

Having just said that meditation is about more than health, perhaps I should confess that I started meditation partly because of something a doctor said to me. I had a minor ailment and went to my doctor expecting an instant remedy in the shape of a bottle of tablets. To my surprise he said that my complaint was the result of stress at work, and he suggested that I take up meditation. I had been vaguely interested in the *idea* of it, but I recall that my reaction to his 'prescription' was one of indignation, that I was perfectly all right as I was! But a seed had been planted, and I slowly did find myself being drawn towards meditation. I bought some books and started trying some meditations. It felt like coming home.

People often expect meditation to be difficult, or to involve some complicated and mysterious process. It doesn't need to. In writing this book I wanted to give a simple meditation which anyone can start straight away. This is the basic breath meditation, which is straightforward to follow but gives an experience of all that meditation is about. The book also gives many other techniques, old and new, and ideas on how meditation can make some very positive differences to your life.

I sincerely hope that you will experience the wonder and beauty that meditation can lead us into. In my own experience meditation is *not* always easy. Sometimes it's really hard to stay still and silent while worldly things beckon for attention. I can only commend it to you as probably the best investment you can make in your own life.

Diana Brueton

1

Understanding What Meditation Is

My advice is to plunge into meditation which gives the keys... to open the door to understanding. To pass from ignorance to knowledge, from the darkness into the light.

George Harrison

You are reading the words on this page. As you do so, are you holding the book, are you sitting down comfortably, are you hot or cold, tired, relaxed, still thinking about what you've just been doing, perhaps wondering about what you may be embarking on? This is the start of meditation. It is all about becoming more aware of *everything* with which you are involved, becoming more conscious of thoughts, physical sensations, feelings and the innermost parts of your self. It is a tried and tested way to:

- still the mind
- relax the body
- create inner harmony.

LOOKING AT MEDITATION

Meditation has been used in almost all major religions, including Christianity, although it is mostly associated with Buddhism and Hinduism. But in recent years it has become less attached to any particular religion or sect. Nowadays it's not just monks and devotees who meditate, it's anyone. What these 'new meditators' have seen in meditation is a way to:

- cope with the hectic pace of life as it now is
- reconnect with a sense of who we really are
- gain control over thoughts and feelings
- find a sense of peace and calm which helps us deal with life's ups and downs.

Meditation has come West, as Westerners who travelled to the East – where meditation had remained strongest – have discovered its age-old benefits and brought it back with them. Many meditation techniques are either directly taken from or based on ancient Eastern ones, but the delight of meditation is that it also lends itself to being constantly changed. It can be secular as well as spiritual.

That's why in this book you will find traditionally based meditations, such as the **breath meditation** in the next chapter which can be the basis of your practice, alongside ones which include very modern activities – even driving. You can:

- try out meditations which have been used for thousands of years
- use techniques which are particularly aimed at calming the mind and body
- discover meditations which will energise and revitalise
- explore meditations which have direct connections with everyday life.

SEEING WHAT HAPPENS IN MEDITATION

Focusing attention

All meditation techniques have in common the idea that **attention** is all-important. Most of us spend much of the time doing one thing while thinking about a hundred and one others. It is not a very satisfying feeling, it is as though you have missed out on something because your attention was elsewhere. You *have* missed out on something if, say, you go for a walk but your thoughts are still on what happened in the office or what you're going to cook for supper.

Meditation is a way of increasing the attention, of helping you become more aware of what is happening in your

- thoughts
- body
- emotions
- surroundings.

It increases feelings of aliveness by providing a reminder to be alert to what's happening here and now. This is what distinguishes meditation from relaxation, sleep or states such as hypnosis:

- it is a state of being calm yet alert.

Understanding the difference between meditation and concentration

Sometimes meditation and **concentration** are talked of as if they are the same thing. This is not surprising: when you're involved in a task that needs care and thought, you are also giving it attention. In fact meditation and concentration *are* different and any confusion between them probably comes from the words we use to describe them. We just don't have the vocabulary for all the different states of meditation – unlike Hindi, for instance, which has many ways of describing the different experiences you may have. The main differences between the states of meditation and concentration are:

- Meditation is a relaxed process in which the meditator's awareness and attention is all-encompassing.

- Concentration is an intense process in which attention is pinpointed.

- Meditation is *in*clusive – it allows your attention to be given to your thoughts and feelings, to physical sensations, even to smells and sounds.

- Concentration is *ex*clusive – you try hard to keep your thoughts on the task in hand and to block out anything else.

The best way to see the difference is by comparing how you feel at the end of a meditation to how you are after a period of extreme concentration, whether physical or mental.

- Meditation usually leaves you feeling refreshed, alert and relaxed.

- Concentration often leaves you feeling tired, agitated and tense.

Concentration is like a laser beam. It is incisive, and is of great use for carrying out particular jobs, but it is too intense to be sustained for long. Meditation is more like a candle flame. It has a centre of bright light, but the gentle light around it has no real boundary, it moves in the breeze and is restful even when looked at for a long time.

Becoming more alive and alert

As you become more aware of yourself and your actions through meditation, you may experience some changes in your relationship to the world. There can be moments when you *become* the thing you are doing. You dance so intensely that you become the dance and not just the dancer. You smell a rose and for a split second you are one with the rose. Perhaps this is something we are closer to as children, when we play so intently that we really believe that the game we are playing is reality, and yet we can still recognise our mother's voice when she calls us.

Acknowledging spirituality

Meditation has been used as a spiritual practice for thousands of years. For some people this begs the question of what spiritual means. As this has taxed the minds of thousands of wise people for as many years, and prompted the writing of some of the world's most influential and profound books, it might be presumptuous to try to answer that here! The relevant thing about spirituality as you start meditating is what – if anything – it means for *you*. You may:

- be convinced there is nothing beyond this mortal flesh

- have a firm belief in a religion or particular spiritual approach to life

- have an open mind and wish to discover your own truth.

Each of these is a valid approach. By meditating you are likely to deepen your understanding of what you consider to be the spiritual side of life, if any, and how it affects your life. You may prefer just to leave behind such labels, and try meditation for reasons of self-discovery and improved quality of life. Whichever, be prepared for insights and perhaps some surprises along the way.

DECIDING YOU WANT TO MEDITATE

Making the decision to meditate is an important step. It is entering into unknown territory, and you need a few signposts along the way.

How do you meditate?

Meditations can be very straightforward or quite complex. They all have two elements in common:

1. **Focus.** Your focus may be simply the **breath**, or it could be a **mantra** (a single repeated word or phrase), an object, sound or other activity. The focus is where you put your attention in any particular meditation. Each time you find your thoughts have strayed elsewhere, you gently return to the focus. The meditations throughout this book will give you many ideas for how to focus your attention.

2. **Witnessing.** You develop a way of passively disregarding all intrusions, whether from your own thoughts or external sources. You do not try to push them away. Instead you acknowledge them and stay with your focus.

In Figure 1, you will find a checklist of the main components of meditation. You can see how straightforward it is. Follow the outline and adapt the general principles to any meditation.

STARTING TO MEDITATE

A step-by-step guide to help you start meditating. These general principles apply to any meditation, though details may vary

1. **Find a quiet place and sit comfortably.** Ideally this should be a place that you use regularly. This will help you to drop into the meditative state more readily. Try sitting cross-legged on a firm, fairly high cushion, with something soft beneath your feet. Alternatively sit on a straight-backed chair, legs uncrossed and feet firmly on the floor, or on a meditation stool. Rest the hands gently in your lap or on your legs. Except in particular meditations, do not lie down as your body will associate this with sleeping.

2. **Soften and relax.** Close your eyes. Start by breathing out several times with a loud sigh. Enjoy it – it's the body's natural way of releasing tension. Gradually allow your breathing to become slow and easy. Do a mental check through your body, noticing any parts that feel tense. As you breathe out, allow the tension to go too. Note any tensions, and release them, throughout the meditation.

3. **Still your mind.** Depending on what meditation you are doing, keep your attention on the focus – such as the breath, a mantra or an object. If thoughts keep intruding, tell your mind that you are putting these to one side for the moment. Let the focus of the meditation occupy as much of your attention as possible.

4. **Be a witness to your thoughts.** Notice when your thoughts have gone elsewhere. Sometimes it helps to name them. Then let them go, so that all intrusive thoughts are acknowledged then disregarded. Return to the focus, having witnessed your thoughts, feelings and sensations.

5. **Finish meditating gradually**. Bring yourself back to your surroundings slowly so that you do not feel disorientated. Open your eyes when you feel ready, look around you, stretch, feel your feet on the ground.

6. **Meditate daily.** Regular meditation builds up your 'meditation muscle'. It is normal to find that your mind wanders. Regular practice will help and will produce the greatest effects on your life.

Fig.1. Checklist for meditating.

KNOWING THE BENEFITS OF MEDITATION

Meditation covers a range of techniques, which all

- allow a rediscovery of a natural sense of calm
- encourage an altered state of awareness
- create a feeling of coming home to oneself.

These are the emotional and spiritual benefits of meditation, the intangible ones that can only be judged subjectively. They can't really be monitored by scientific devices. But some of the benefits of meditation *can* be monitored, for there is now an extensive body of research which shows the effects on our physiology.

EXAMINING THE EVIDENCE FOR IMPROVED HEALTH

When a claim is made that something can improve health, it is usually subjected to rigorous tests and trials. So why not meditation? We are becoming increasingly aware that modern lifestyles are impairing our health, and are looking for ways of counteracting this, but many people want proof that something like meditation can help. Although meditation would not seem to lend itself readily to the kind of research and clinical trials that a new drug might undergo, a body of research has gradually emerged. The results – and their effects – have been surprisingly dramatic.

Researching the benefits

In the late 1960s an American researcher, Herbert Benson, was studying high blood pressure in monkeys. Some people who had started doing transcendental meditation asked him if he would study them. His initial reaction was that he shouldn't get involved in something so off-beat: 'It was 1968 and it was Harvard Medical School. I was having difficulties even trying to convince my colleagues stress might be related to hypertension (high blood pressure).'

Eventually Benson succumbed, and he and other independent researchers at the University of California discovered that our bodies have what he called a 'relaxation response', which can be induced by meditation. However, he also thought that this response wasn't unique to meditation but could also arise from prayer, breathing exercises, and even the repetitive motion of jogging. It took time for the specific benefits of meditation to be pin-pointed further.

Over the next years the research was taken up by many other people, and claims were made that meditation could affect a wide range of conditions including:

- sleep disorders

- anxiety

- high blood pressure

- muscular tension

- high cholesterol

- stress.

Getting to the heart of the matter

Some of the claims were quite astonishing – at least to the medical world. For instance, in the UK a group of people considered to be at risk of severe heart problems were taught meditation and relaxation techniques. After four years their health was compared with members of a control group who had not meditated. The results, showing the meditators were at much less risk of high blood pressure, heart attack or stroke than the non-meditators, were published in the *British Medical Journal*. This was just one of many such trials. A hospital at the University of Massachusetts was even moved to start a meditation clinic, to which thousands of patients have been referred for a wide range of illnesses. However, despite the growing mass of evidence, medical practitioners were wary of prescribing a dose of meditation for their patients' ills.

Dr Dean Ornish's breakthrough

The turning point for the Western world's acceptance of meditation as a means to a healthier way of life came in 1990. American cardiologist Dr Dean Ornish presented his findings to an incredulous press. He showed that not only was it possible to prevent or slow down heart disease, but that it was actually possible to *reverse* the process. In a country where cardiac illness is a top killer, this was big news. Ornish's results were particularly impressive as they made use of the latest high-tech imaging through which the diameter of blood vessels could be measured; his results were later published in the leading UK medical journal, *The Lancet*, and *Time* magazine commented that 'by normal standards, the impossible had happened'.

Ornish's findings were simplicity itself. He proved that heart disease could be not only prevented but also reversed by:

- taking moderate exercise
- following a low-fat diet
- and *meditating regularly.*

His evidence was so compelling that major cardiology centres across America, such as a New York teaching hospital, started offering this programme and one of the world's largest insurance companies immediately announced they would reimburse the medical fees of anyone participating in such a programme. The message could no longer be ignored, when top doctors in some of the world's most advanced medical centres started saying that it would be malpractice if they did not offer meditation for heart disease.

The UK message

In 1993 well over one hundred British doctors wrote to the Secretary of State for Health. They were asking for **transcendental meditation** (TM) to be made available on the NHS, and claimed this could save millions of pounds a year. They pointed to evidence from Canada, where it was shown that the cost of health care for 677 people who learnt TM was almost halved within seven years.

How *does* meditation help physical conditions?

The **fight-or-flight response** is a familiar idea – the body's natural response to stress. Some researchers reasoned that if the body has an automatic response to stressful situations which helps survival, it might also have a natural response to do with recovering and recuperating. Could this be, they wondered, what meditation is about? Perhaps meditation is the body's natural balance to stress – the **relaxation response**, Figure 2. In meditation the body's metabolism changes:

- alpha brainwaves increase
- the heart rate slows
- blood pressure drops
- oxygen consumption goes down
- the metabolic rate decreases
- and muscular tension is released.

But why not just relax and take a nap, and wait for all these things to happen of their own accord? Because all of these changes, which make

THE RELAXATION RESPONSE

Dr Herbert Benson coined the phrase 'the relaxation response'. This table summarises what he found when he investigated the physical effects of different relaxation techniques and meditations

Technique	Oxygen consumption	Respiratory rate	Heart rate	Alpha waves	Blood pressure	Muscle tension
Transcendental meditation	Decreases	Decreases	Decreases	Increases	Decreases	Not measured
Zen and Yoga	Decreases	Decreases	Decreases	Increases	Decreases	Not measured
Autogenic training	Not measured	Decreases	Decreases	Increases	Inconclusive	Decreases
Progressive relaxation	Not measured	Not measured	Not measured	Not measured	Inconclusive	Decreases
Hypnosis with suggested deep relaxation	Decreases	Decreases	Decreases	Not measured	Inconclusive	Not measured

Fig. 2. The physical effects of meditation and relaxation techniques.

you feel good, happen at a *much faster* rate than when you just sit and take a break. And the changes that happen in the brain during meditation are of a quite different sort to anything that happens during sleep or rest. We move away from beta brainwaves, which are to do with thinking and everyday occupations, and into **alpha waves** which are experienced as a state of well-being and calm. If we go even deeper we access the theta wavelength, a state of dreaminess.

How does this happen? Electroencephalograph (EEG) tests show that it's all to do with the brain. The brain has two sides:

- the left side of the brain is usually dominant, dealing with verbal, analytical and rational thought processes
- the right side of the brain deals more with emotion, creativity, intuition.

In meditation the left side of the brain gives way to the right side, which now becomes more active. It seems that a rebalancing of the brain happens, which allows the body to return to equilibrium, and in particular for the immune system to be boosted. It is tempting to speculate that we might have been 'designed' to have periods of what we now call meditation, in order for the body to recover from times of fight-or-flight or general exertion.

The latest research
Researchers seem to be fascinated by what happens in meditation. One of the most recent studies (1998) was carried out at Copenhagen University. EEG measurements proved that meditation is a different state from either wakefulness or sleep. The brain's theta rhythm slows down but the alpha rhythm remains. The researcher of the project concluded that meditation is 'A balance between activity and non-activity. You become receptive'. He also noted an increase in meditators' use of the imagination, and suggested that meditation could even be used to treat severe mental disorders as well as 'stopping the separation between mind, body and spirit' in 'well' people.

Helping with other illnesses
Most of the initial research into the medical benefits of meditation dealt with conditions related to stress and, particularly, the heart. Since then the net has widened, and meditation has been investigated as a way of helping a much wider range of conditions. This is partly the result of our greater understanding of the mind–body connection. The effects of thoughts and feelings on our metabolism have now been proved. Through this work meditation has now been shown to help conditions such as:

● asthma

● immune dysfunctions

● depression

● some addictions

● arthritis

● migraine

● irritable bowel syndrome

● ME.

Meditation and ageing
Could meditation affect the ageing process? A research project published in the *International Journal of Neuroscience* suggests that it might. The study looked at people in their 50's who had been meditating for five years. In terms of health they were 12 years younger than

non-meditators of the same age. It seems that we are at an exciting time where the benefits of an ancient art are being looked at in the analytical light of science, and being proven. Such proof may not matter to those meditators who already know what a difference it makes to their lives, but it has opened the way for looking at the effects it can have on some very serious conditions, as well as on the quality of life generally.

QUESTIONS AND ANSWERS

I don't have any particular spiritual belief. Would meditation still have anything to offer me?
It certainly could. Many of the people who took part in research into the physical effects of meditation were doing so for the sake of their health, rather than out of any religious or spiritual convictions, and they still benefitted. You might even be in good company. Meditation plays a particularly strong role in Buddhism – many modern techniques are based on Buddhist methods – and yet Buddhism claims to have no belief in God. Your reasons for meditating are as valid as anyone else's.

So is meditation a spiritual practice or a medical treatment?
We now know that mind and body are part of one system. Processes in the brain have an absolutely direct effect on health. Vasu Mitra, a meditation teacher at the London Buddhist Centre, explains it this way: 'Meditation is a spiritual discipline that can also benefit medical conditions. It aims to unite mind and body, which is essential to any healing process. It takes the neurosis out of living and gives you peace of mind, and the body naturally rights itself … It educates the emotions, helps you to live in the present and be happy. Happiness isn't just down to chance – you can develop it.'

SUMMARY

1. Meditation is a simple and enjoyable way of finding inner calm through becoming aware of thoughts, feelings and what is happening around us.

2. By taking our attention to a particular focus in meditation, we become both more alert to life and more relaxed within ourselves.

3. The benefits to our physical health have now been conclusively proved, and there is strong evidence of the positive effects on our mental and emotional health.

2

Establishing a Basic Meditation

If you can do something with the breath, you will suddenly turn to the present. If you can do something with breath, you will attain to the source of life. If you can do something with breath, you can transcend time and space. if you can do something with breath, you will be in the world and also beyond it.

Osho

This chapter shows you how to do a meditation which will form the basis of your practice. You will be able to come back to it whenever you want to, whatever other meditations you choose to try out as well.

This meditation – or variations on it – is probably the most widespread form of meditation there is. It is very simple, costs nothing to do, and can be the best thing in your life that you ever discovered. The basic meditation will help you:

- find greater calm

- feel more in control in your life

- develop an inner core of peacefulness.

A simple meditation such as this could be called the ultimate holiday: you can take it at any time and anywhere.

BEGINNING SIMPLY

The technique is beautifully straightforward. It is based on something you have access to at all times and in all places – *your own breath.*

Using the breath to meditate

Meditation can make use of anything to help develop attention – it does not have to be the breath. However, the advantages of using the breath are:

- As the breath is within us, it helps to acknowledge what is happening inside us.

● It is always available.

● It is the life-giving force, and bringing awareness to it can be helpful physically, mentally and spiritually.

● It can be very calming.

In Yogic teachings it is said that we are born with a given number of breaths. While this may or may not be literally true, it does say something about the importance of the breath, and how by connecting with it we are also connecting with the life within us.

Feeling the breath
Where do you feel your breath – on the tip of your nose, the back of your throat, in your chest? It is in all of those places, and more. In the meditation you will become aware of the breath moving through all of these parts of the body, but then you will gradually focus on one particular point. This is the place to which your thoughts will be continually encouraged to return.

STILLING YOURSELF

The following meditation on the breath is usually done for an hour. It is very valuable to do it for this long, but if you are unable to find this amount of time, doing it for half an hour or even just ten minutes is good too. Doing meditation *regularly* is the key.

As you will need to have your eyes closed during the meditation, read through the instructions beforehand until you have absorbed them well enough to relax into the meditation. Alternatively, record yourself reading the instructions for the meditation, set out in Figure 3, and play the tape back as you meditate.

Starting the meditation

Most but not all meditations are done sitting down. This is one of them. Find a place and position to sit where you will be:

● undisturbed

● comfortable

● as upright as possible

● at ease

● unlikely to fall asleep.

THE BASIC BREATH MEDITATION

Listening to your own voice is the very best way of instructing yourself. Record the tape so that it lasts about an hour, leaving plenty of time between each reminder

Settle down comfortably.
Close your eyes.
Take a few deep breaths, let the breath go ...
Feel any tensions in the body.
Breathe into them, release them ...
Let the shoulders drop.
Feel the spine lengthening upwards.
Let your face loosen.
Allow the tongue to become relaxed in the mouth.
The breath is getting deeper ...
Soften any tension ...
Feel the breath coming in through your nose ...
And out ...
Now feel the breath right down through the throat, the chest and into the lower abdomen. Find that point in the abdomen where it rises and falls ...
Stay with feeling the breath there ...
Soften any tension ...
Come back to the breath ...
Let go of any tension ...
And return to the breath ...
Return to the breath ...
[continue repeating this at ever longer intervals]

A few minutes before ending:
Let your breathing get a bit slower and deeper.
Listen to what is happening around you. Move your head and neck a little, now your hands, your body.
In a minute it will be time to open your eyes and look around.
Come back gently, enjoying the meditative space you have created and knowing you can return to it at any time.

Fig. 3. Making a tape for the basic breath meditation.

The ideal position is sitting cross-legged on a firm cushion on the ground, as this automatically puts the spine in an upright position. If this is too uncomfortable for you, then sitting on a straight-backed chair, with legs uncrossed and feet on the ground, is a perfectly good alternative. In Chapter 3 we will look further at how, where and when to sit for meditation; for now, get started by settling into whichever sitting position you have chosen.

Starting to move within

- Settle onto your cushion or chair, feeling your body in contact with it.

- Rest your hands on your legs in a relaxed and easy position.

- Take a minute to look around you, noticing where you are as though with new eyes.

- When you feel settled, close your eyes.

- Take several deep breaths, letting the air out as though you're sighing. Enjoy the feeling of letting go of any rushing around you've been doing.

- Allow your shoulders to relax and drop, and at the same time feel your spine very gently lengthening, as though a string attached to the top of your head is being pulled upward.

- Slowly let the breathing settle back down into its natural rhythm.

- Start to become aware of your body. Notice any places where you feel particularly tense or stiff, and let them melt and soften a little.

- Take a few minutes to get used to sitting here with your eyes closed. Can you feel the weight of your body on the floor or chair, do you notice your breath, any particular parts of the body – maybe even the beating of your heart?

- Enjoy the sensations in your body, and remain relaxed yet alert.

MEDITATING ON THE BREATH – THE BASIC MEDITATION

You have now moved from the outer world to the inner. It is as though a sea anemone might withdraw its tentacles so that everything is concentrated inside rather than out, or as though you have put a cloak around you and all your attention is for the time being within you. Now it is time to start to become more aware of your breath, to let it be the focus for your meditation.

Step I

● Feel the breath coming into your nose. Notice how it is slightly cold as it enters the nostrils. Allow yourself the luxury of tracing its progress right down the back of your throat, then swelling the chest. See how the whole of your abdomen expands too, how your shoulders move apart slightly, and your stomach rises and fills out.

● Now trace the breath as it leaves the body. The stomach drops, the chest contracts and you may feel the warmed breath coming up the throat, down the nostrils and leaving the body. Feels its warmth on the tip of your nose.

The first few times you do the meditation, take about five minutes to get to know your breath in this way. You may feel it as a kind of circle, a repeating pattern. Try to let the breathing stay as natural as possible. Get to know every nook and cranny of its journey through your body, including how it spreads out to the more far-flung corners. Can you feel your breath even down in your feet, or in your fingers?

Step 2

Now you are ready to focus your attention on just one point in the body where the breath is felt strongly.

● In your mind's eye find a place within your lower abdomen where you feel the rise and fall of the air. It is usually felt most clearly an inch or two above the navel (hence the old term contemplating your navel!).

● It may help to place your hand over this area for a while to help you get used to feeling the stomach rising and falling.

The reason for choosing this part of the body to locate the breath is that:

    – the breath is felt particularly strongly in the lower abdomen
    – the abdomen is often considered the centre of our being
    – the abdomen provides a clear-cut point to focus on.

Step 3

● Stay with allowing your attention to be on this focal point, the place you have identified in the abdomen where you feel the breath.

- Each time you notice that your attention has gone elsewhere, gently usher yourself back to that point.

- Realising that your thoughts were elsewhere will happen frequently! Do not be hard on yourself, rather be grateful that you have noticed.

- When you are able to, let go of the thought or feeling. Let it drift off, like a passing cloud or a morning mist, and return to the point of the breath in the abdomen.

- Notice where your attention has gone to

- and return to the breath.

- Notice where your attention has gone to

- and return to the breath.

- And so on until the end of the meditation.

It is important not to force this. Take note of what was happening, rather than telling yourself off for letting your attention wander. Be a gentle shepherd with your thoughts, rather than a ringmaster cracking the whip.

Becoming aware of the pattern of your breathing
Have you ever noticed the cycle of your breathing pattern? We breathe in and we breathe out, but there is also a still point where nothing seems to be happening, between the 'in-out' and then between the 'out-in' parts of the cycle. You may notice this more as you start to be more attuned to your breathing and its pattern. Try to become as aware of these still points as of the breaths themselves.

Step 4
It helps if you have some way of letting yourself know when your time for meditation is nearing an end. Try setting an alarm clock, or asking someone to let you know.

- Finish the meditation gradually. Allow the breath to deepen and take a few strong breaths in and out.

- Listen to any noises around you, inside or outside the room.

- Start to gently move your body, stretching legs, arms, hands and neck.

- When you are ready open your eyes. Take a few minutes to look around and reorientate yourself.

- Make sure you are back in touch with the physical world! When you stand up feel your feet firmly connected to the ground, and start moving gradually and deliberately.

- Thank yourself for giving yourself this time, and resolve to return to that inner space again.

ADDING TO THE BASIC TECHNIQUE

There are several additions or changes you can make to this technique. Some of them are ones you might want to try out just a few times, as they are aids to getting the hang of the meditation. Others are slight variations which you may find work better for you. See what suits you best.

Helping to attune to the breath

Counting
For the first ten minutes or so of attuning to the breath, count each in-breath from one to four. Then return to one, count up to four and continue like this. However, each time you notice that your thoughts have been elsewhere, start counting from one again. You may be surprised at how often you have to go back to one! This is helpful in keeping your attention on the breath.

Naming
After doing the counting technique, move on to the technique of **naming**. You are now focusing as much as possible on the breath; each time you realise that your thoughts have been elsewhere, quickly give them a name. It can be something very general, such as 'sadness', 'food', 'uncomfortable' – anything that comes into your mind. Once you have named it you can then choose to let go of it and return to the breath. Naming is another way of becoming more aware of where your preoccupations are, but not getting caught up in them.

Variations on the theme

Focusing on the end of the nose
Instead of placing your attention in the abdomen, try focusing on the very tip of your nose throughout the meditation. Feel the difference in temperature between the in and out breaths.

Focusing between the eyes
Let the point where you feel the breath be between the eyes, as though

at the very top of the nasal passage. This is also a traditional place to focus attention. Notice if it has a different affect on you from when you focus on the abdomen.

Sharpening awareness

A student of meditation was practising in an ancient monastery. Sitting alone in his monk's cell, doing meditation on the breath, he heard a bird land on the windowsill outside. Talking to his teacher later, he proudly announced that he had noticed he had heard the bird land at exactly the moment his breath was still. 'Very good,' replied his master, 'but was it the stillness between the in-breath and the out-breath, or between the out-breath and the in-breath?'

The student realised he still had some way to go before he could boast of his awareness.

QUIETENING THE MIND

Sometimes it can feel as though thoughts and feelings are like a runaway train. They can seem to have a life of their own which takes over everything else – including keeping the attention on the breath.

Witnessing

One of the keys to meditation is noticing what is happening in thoughts and feelings. This is known as **witnessing**. Each time you spot that you have been away in some chain of thinking, remembering, imagining or whatever, just take note of that. Be a witness to your thoughts. You are not making any judgements on those thoughts, you are simply saying to yourself that at this moment you notice them, but you choose to return to having your attention on the breath.

This is an idea which you will come back to many times in learning meditation. While meditating, you are an impartial witness to whatever you are thinking or feeling. You notice where your attention has gone, acknowledge it, and move on – in this case back to the breath.

QUESTIONS AND ANSWERS

How do I know if I'm doing it right?
This is a question which can be a real torment at times, whatever meditation you're doing, so it's good to tackle it right from the start. The answer is that there is not really a 'right' way, in that everyone's experience is going to differ and it is impossible to really compare

experiences. Take comfort, though, from the fact that many, many people have used this meditation before you, have no doubt gone through similar doubts and have gone on to feel the benefits of meditation. Through their experience they have devised methods which we know do 'work'. Keep following the guidelines and trust in your own ability to get it more 'right' all the time. Being human, practice may never make perfect, but it certainly helps!

Sometimes my breathing feels very tight and uncomfortable. Is this meditation likely to make it worse?
No, it's likely to make it better. However, it may take a while to relax into it, so initially it may give you the sensation of being worse. This is because you are now giving your breathing attention, there is no escape from it into other distractions and you may be even more aware than usual of any tension in it. Reassure yourself that it will change, and steadily allow the breaths to get deeper and slower. Notice what thoughts or feelings are associated with the tightness, then let them go and come back to the life-giving breath again.

I only seem to be able to keep my thoughts on the breath for a very short time, then realise I have been miles away for ages.
This is the human condition! None of us is different, but you may find that with practice the time you are able to stay with the breath before thoughts intervene gets longer. Have the courage to stick with it rather than giving up in frustration. However, even after meditating for a long time you will probably find that some days are easier than others. That's natural – your body goes through different rhythms, and different things are happening in your life. Meditating can help put these in some perspective.

I'm not used to sitting cross-legged on the floor, and find it very uncomfortable. Is sitting in a chair as good?
Yes. It is best not to lie down to meditate, as this will give your body the wrong message and you are likely to lose awareness. Sitting in a firm chair, where you can remain both comfortable and alert, is fine.

SUMMARY

1. Establishing a straightforward meditation can be the basis of your meditation practice. Using one based on the breath has many benefits. It can be used in almost any circumstance, and is a tried and tested way of moving into meditation.

2. Set yourself up for your meditation so that you are comfortable but alert. Take time to settle down, to move gradually from the outer world to the inner. Focus more and more deeply on the breath, coming back to it whenever possible. Try out variations, such as counting the breath and naming your thoughts.

3. Enjoy the new experiences. Let it be a pleasure, find ways of incorporating it into our life and notice any effects it is having.

3

Setting Up a Regular Practice

Meditation is a way to cultivate sanity and well-being and wisdom in one's life that you can't get from watching television or taking a pill.
Jon Kabat-Zinn, University of Massachusetts Medical Center

MAKING A DECISION TO MEDITATE

Now you have a flavour of what meditation is about. If it was at times difficult to keep your attention focused as much as you would like, consider the positive parts of your experience. Did you at any time have a feeling of calmness, an insight, some kind of unexpected or revealing sensation? Think about whether these glimpses are sufficient to encourage you to make a commitment to meditating on a regular basis.

Choosing to embark on meditation

What are your reasons for meditation? To arrive at a point where you feel ready to make an ongoing commitment, it may be helpful to assess what you want or hope for from it. You might be looking for:

● time away from everyday concerns

● a way of connecting with your inner self

● a deepening of your religious or spiritual practice

● time to be quiet and peaceful

● a drug-free way of helping a physical condition

● something which you feel is missing in your life at present

● a way of untangling the knot of thoughts and feelings

● greater calm.

Do any of these ring a bell? Maybe there are other needs particular to you, which you would like to address through meditation. It is helpful to have some idea about this, in order to strengthen your commitment. But you're also quite likely to find that other benefits emerge as you progress. For instance, a woman who took up meditation to reduce her high blood pressure not only succeeded in doing this but also found that through meditating her relationships with her family became much calmer.

This is a journey into uncharted territory. Many people have been along the same route using the same methods, but as it is a journey into *your* self it is going to be new at every step.

ESTABLISHING A PRACTICE

Time to firm up your resolve! By meditating as frequently as possible you are more likely to:

● go more deeply into the meditation

● make it a real and continuing part of your life

● find it gets easier all the time – like an athlete building up muscle, you build up 'meditative muscle' by practising frequently

● be able to meditate more easily at particularly stressful or difficult times

● get in touch with the calm, meditative space during everyday life.

Give some thought to how much time you can realistically dedicate to meditation at the moment.

Checking out what is possible

To get clearer about what is feasible for you, within all the demands on your life as it is now, try asking yourself these questions.

1. What are my reasons for choosing to meditate?

2. Why might I find it difficult to meditate regularly?

3. How could I start to overcome these difficulties?

4. Realistically, how frequently could I meditate?

    For.............................minutes/hours per day
    On...............................days per week
    For a total of...............hours per week

5. Unrealistically, how frequently would I *like* to meditate?

    For.............................minutes/hours per day
    On...............................days per week
    For a total of...............hours per week

6. When could I start following a meditation programme, based on my realistic figures?

Following a programme

One good way of starting is to use one particular meditation regularly for a certain period of time – 28 days is often recommended as it gives you time to experience it quite deeply and to feel the changes it can bring about. For instance, you could:

● try out the basic meditation from the previous chapter for 28 days

● then follow this up by trying some of the other meditations in the following chapters.

This programme would be particularly appropriate for someone starting meditation.

If you are more experienced, or simply can't wait to try out some other techniques, you could equally well commit yourself to a certain period of meditating, but using a variety of methods. You might decide to:

● use the basic meditation for seven days

● then try a new meditation for seven days

● return to the basic meditation for seven days

● and so on.

If time is not a problem you could even do *two* meditations a day, giving you a wide range of options. Again, ask yourself:

1. How many days can I set myself for following an initial meditation programme, considering all my other commitments?

2. What meditation(s) would I like to start with?

3. Would I prefer to use just one meditation during this time, or several?

Sample programmes

The following are just some possibilities for how you might devise a meditation programme.

Programme 1
Early morning. Basic breath meditation, half an hour.
Early evening. Basic breath meditation, half an hour.

Follow this programme for 28 days, then start introducing new meditations in the evening.

Programme 2
Early morning. Any of the revitalising meditations from Chapter 7. Time as appropriate.
Lunch time. Basic breath meditation. Ten minutes.
Early evening. Basic breath meditation. Half an hour.

Programme 3
Early morning. Basic breath meditation. Ten minutes.
Early evening. Any of the stress-releasing meditations from Chapter 6. One hour.

Programme 4
Basic breath meditation, one hour, *either* early morning or evening.

Programme 5
Alternate days basic breath meditation/other meditations. A good way of trying new techniques whilst retaining the basic method.

Programme 6
Your own programme, devised to fit your circumstances.

CHOOSING WHEN, WHERE AND HOW

Once you have decided you are going to make a commitment to meditate you will want to consider when and where to do it. Meditation can be done anywhere. You might even say that one of the aims of practising regularly is so that you *can* meditate on the bus, in the back garden, standing in the supermarket queue or wherever. But for most of us this is something to build up over time. The idea of 'meditative muscle' is a useful one – the more meditation you do, the more familiar it becomes. It may not necessarily become easier – even the most experienced meditators still have their difficult days – but it will deepen and you will know the benefits of sticking to it. That's why it's useful when building up a meditation practice to establish:

- a regular time

- a regular place, including perhaps a special place used only for meditation

- a routine.

FINDING THE RIGHT TIME

Any time of the day is suitable for meditation if that time is right for you. Again you need to consider the practicalities of demands on your time and when you're least likely to be disturbed. There are, though, certain times of the day that have traditionally been used for meditation, as they are particularly conducive to entering a meditative state.

Working with the body's natural energies

You might like to give special consideration to meditating either:

● in the early morning

● or the early evening.

These are particularly good times. You are less likely to have other demands on you, such as work, and will probably be more relaxed.

Meditating in the early morning
Early in the morning you can still be carrying some of that inner world of sleep and dreams with you. This relaxed state means that you will find this a potent time to tune into your self. The other benefit of meditating at this time is that it makes a big difference to the day ahead. It establishes a calm state that affects your reactions and interactions. Try it, and see if your day seems smoother, that you are more in tune with yourself and your activities throughout it.

Meditating in the evening
In the evening your body may be more tired, allowing you to relax into your inner self. This is also a good time to let go of the things that have happened during the day, thus giving you a kind of mental and emotional cleansing before sleeping. Dusk, when day is giving way to night, is a particularly potent time. You naturally start to move into a more reflective, receptive state as light gives way to dark.

As with the morning meditation, you will also find that it has an effect on what lies ahead – in this case, slowing down and sleeping. (See also meditations designed specifically for entering sleep, pages 71–74.)

SETTING UP A MEDITATION SPACE

Just as in theory you can meditate at any *time*, so you can meditate any*where* – but in practice some places are better than others. We all know how certain places can affect the way we feel. You can make use of this to help you with your meditation. Although the aim is to gradually bring meditation into daily life, certain practices can help to develop that state. Creating a **meditation** or **sacred space** is one such technique.

HAVING A PARTICULAR MEDITATION PLACE

If you are able to do your regular practice in the same place, this can help you to enter more quickly into meditation. Your mind will immediately associate that place with the activity you do there, and so be more immediately prepared for it. If this sounds implausible, think about how differently you feel on going into, for instance, a school, a church, a workplace, a hospital, a sports hall. You connect certain activities or even emotions with these places, and respond accordingly.

Your meditation space may be a whole room if you have that luxury. It might be a corner of a room that you feel comfortable in, or even a particular chair that you move around as necessary.

Creating an atmosphere
Your meditation space could include all or some of the following:

- a comfortable cushion or chair

- a candle

- a vase of flowers

- a picture of someone you associate with meditation, such as a spiritual teacher, if appropriate to you

- perhaps a small natural 'treasure' you have found, such as a stone or shell

- any object that is precious as a reminder of being still and in touch with yourself

- an essential oil burner or incense holder if this appeals to you.

These might be set up in a permanent place, in which case you also have the benefit of being reminded of meditation whenever you see them during the day. Otherwise, setting them up before the meditation can become part of your meditation, giving a message to yourself about what you are about to do.

GETTING PRACTICAL ABOUT YOUR ROUTINE

There are other ways in which you can prepare yourself for meditation. None of them need take very long, but they will all help set the tone and mood for what you are about to enter into. They give you the message that this is a precious time, one that is worth while preparing for. They are also another way of building up a routine which, by just doing it regularly, can give you an instant way into the right frame of mind.

Preparing yourself for meditation

Cleansing
Many religious traditions set great store by preparing the body for religious practices, through washing. There is both practical and symbolic point to this. By bathing or showering before meditation you:

● make a cut-off point between your everyday activities and your meditation

● make a symbolic statement about your intention in meditating

● feel physically refreshed.

If it is not practical to bath or shower, wash your hands prior to meditation. Do it as consciously as possible, feeling the practical concerns of your day being washed away.

Clothing
Wear loose, comfortable clothing. Make sure you will be warm enough,

as you may well cool down if you are sitting for any length of time. You might have a light shawl or jumper within reach in case this happens. If possible wear clothes made of natural materials such as wool or cotton so that your body can breathe fully It is useful to keep certain clothes for meditating in, simply because they feel right, but there is no need to be too rigid about this.

Certain colours have been traditionally associated with meditation: Buddhists dress in saffron and maroon robes, yogis often wear white and so on. Wear whatever colour you feel right in, but try giving it some thought and see if it makes any difference to you. What does it feel like, for instance, to meditate wearing black as compared with white, or green compared with deep red? Colours do affect us, and can be used to enhance your meditation.

Food and drink
Just as when you take physical exercise, it is best to avoid meditating very soon after eating. You are likely to be drowsy, so if possible leave an hour or so after eating any large amount before meditating. On the other hand, don't be hungry or you will get distracted and be able to think of nothing but food. Balance is all, as in so many aspects of meditation.

The same applies to drink. Make sure you won't be thirsty, but also don't drink too much beforehand for obvious reasons. Opinion is divided on what, if anything you should drink. One school of thought advises abstaining from any stimulating drinks, including tea and coffee. There again, it is said that tea was actually discovered by a meditator who found it made him much more alert.

Choosing what to sit on
There are three main choices for your meditation seat:

- A firm cushion. It should be high enough to raise your spine upright and so that your weight is not resting on your ankles.

- An upright chair. Make sure your feet are firmly on the floor, if necessary put something underneath them rather than leave them dangling.

- A meditation stool. These are specially designed stools in which your knees are also in contact with the floor as you sit astride the stool (see Figure 4). They are much more comfortable than they sound, and help the back to straighten.

Whether you prefer to meditate sitting on ...

a cushion ...

an upright chair ...

or a meditation stool, allow your spine to be upright but relaxed.

Fig. 4. Sitting positions for meditation.

Preparing the place for meditation

Whether you are meditating in a special meditation space or elsewhere, try to ensure that the place is:

● warm but not over-heated

● well-ventilated

● somewhere where you will not be disturbed.

Creating a setting-up ritual
Preparing the place for meditation need take only a few moments but is important for what follows. Create your own 'rituals' as you go. This may be simply closing the door to a room which is normally open to all, lighting a candle or setting your chair or cushion in place.

This is also valuable if you are meditating away from your usual place. One meditator whose work means he has to travel a lot always buys a bunch of flowers to place in his hotel room, as a way of creating an atmosphere for meditation in an anonymous place.

QUESTIONS AND ANSWERS

I can't imagine my children giving me the time and quiet I'd need to meditate regularly ... and then the phone's always ringing. Shouldn't I put my needs to one side for the time being?
Perhaps having your needs met would benefit the whole family. Being meditative would give you a space where you could unload all the demands of parenthood for a while. It could also set the children an example which would help them in their own lives one day. There are ways of finding at least small spaces of time for yourself, such as a time of day when all the family is out, in a lunch break if you're also working, or by making an ongoing arrangement with your partner. The phone can wait! An added benefit of having a regular time when you meditate is that people *will* gradually come to know about it if you yourself are clear that you do not want to be disturbed, that this is time for you.

It's not practical for me to have a permanent meditation space. I need to be more flexible – are there any other means of support?
You can create a meditation space wherever you are simply by having the intention to do so. Help this along a bit by making the place in which you are meditating special in some way. Place some flowers there if you can. Have a small 'talisman', such as a crystal or special object, that you can have by you and which is associated with meditation. Make use of

smells, such as aromatic oils, to give you an instant whiff of meditation! Olibanum and sandalwood are especially useful.

I know I need to sit as still as possible during meditation, but what if I get an itch?
There will be times when the need to move feels very pressing, whether it's to scratch an itch or because you are uncomfortable. There are two schools of thought on this. One is that you should resist the temptation to move as it is a distraction to your meditation, and just to keep your awareness on the physical sensation. The other is that it is much more important to be comfortable and relaxed. The choice is yours, but you might also consider a 'middle way' – keeping your attention on the sensation until such time as you really must move, but then making sure that you do it with awareness. This may seem like an unimportant question, but it says a lot about how we can bring a meditative attitude to all our thoughts and actions.

SUMMARY

Bear in mind the words of Jonathan Hinde, spokesperson for TM in the UK:

Meditation is not something you do when the need arises, like taking an aspirin for a headache. It must be part of your daily routine, like brushing your teeth.

4

Using Traditional Meditations

The self is not the individual body or mind, but rather that aspect deep inside each individual person that knows the Truth.

Swami Vishnu Devananda

WITNESSING YOUR THOUGHTS AND FEELINGS

By noticing – or witnessing – what you are thinking, feeling and experiencing without judging it or trying to change it, you are increasing your awareness of:

● what thoughts are preoccupying you at the moment

● how your body is feeling

● your mood.

Experiencing witnessing

Witnessing is like being a spectator at a movie – but in this case the movie is all about *you*. Watch what's going on in the movie of your own mind as you meditate. When you notice that you have got caught up in the fast-moving action on the 'screen' in your mind, come back to being the spectator again.

Applying witnessing to other meditations

Witnessing is the essence of all the meditations that follow.

- This chapter adds to the basic breath meditation with more breath-based methods
- Chapter 5 introduces some more meditation techniques
- Chapter 6 has meditations which can be particularly helpful in creating calmness
- Chapter 7 describes meditations to raise energy levels and to bring meditation into everyday life.

At the root of all the techniques, however active or passive, easy or unusual they are, is the idea of increasing awareness through bearing witness to all aspects of your self.

EXPLORING TRADITIONAL BREATHING MEDITATIONS

Many of the traditional forms of meditation come from Buddhism. The ones outlined in this and the next section – vipassana, metta bhavana, zazen – have in recent years formed the basis of much of the meditation that is practised in the West, and do not require knowledge or experience of Buddhism. The names of these methods may seem unusual, but the meditations themselves will soon feel familiar as they are all based in something very familiar – your own body and breath.

Vipassana meditation

If you have tried the basic breath meditation, then you are already doing one version of **vipassana**, which is at the root of many methods. The three main ways of using it are described below.

First method

This is where you attune to the breath in the belly. This is considered to be a particularly powerful point to focus on because it is the root of life, where we were connected to our mothers, and thus the breath is felt particularly strongly here (see Chapter 2).

Second method

You are still attuning to the breath, but this time at the point on the tip of the nose where it enters and leaves the body (see Chapter 2). Some people prefer this way.

Third method

In this method you do not focus your attention on anything particular, you simply become aware of whatever you are doing. You become alert to your legs moving as you walk, to the sounds you hear, to all the sensations in your body and your thoughts. You may also come across this method referred to as **mindfulness meditation**.

Practising vipassana

Any of the three methods can be practised either alone or in any combination. Experiment, use it playfully and with enjoyment. Follow the outline for the basic breath meditation for all of the methods.

As vipassana is such a still meditation it can be difficult to maintain alertness. In Buddhist monasteries this has been overcome by the meditation master wielding a 'Zen stick'. This is tapped on the head of the meditating monks, serving not just to keep them awake but also as a way of inducing instant awareness, an opening into something deeper. You probably don't have access to a meditation master with a Zen stick, so you can:

● occasionally give yourself a mental 'hit' by sharply bringing your attention back to the here and now

● keep yourself alert and awake by incorporating the **walking vipassana** method outlined below.

Walking vipassana
Intersperse sitting vipassana with walking for about 20 or 30 minutes. You simply walk very slowly and deliberately, in a circle or a straight line, with the focus of your attention being on the feet rather than on the breath. Again, allow your thoughts to go elsewhere as necessary, then bring them gently back to your feet. Notice the contact of your feet on the floor, of your body turning, of the movement in the legs. Walk extremely slowly. The benefit of walking as well as sitting is that it keeps you awake, prevents the body from stiffening up and provides a way of bringing your inner meditation into a more everyday activity.

This is also sometimes called **mindfulness of walking**. It can be practised in its own right too, as well as in conjunction with sitting vipassana.

TRYING OTHER TRADITIONAL MEDITATIONS

Buddhist heart meditation (metta bhavana)
The **metta bhavana**, or development of **loving kindness**, focuses the attention on a happy moment, bringing it into the present and extending it to yourself and others.

This is usually done for an hour, but you can make it a length of time to suit you. Make sure, though, that each section is given about the same amount of time.

Step 1
Before the meditation begins, think of three people:

1. A person you love.

2. Someone who you feel fairly indifferent about.

3. Somebody towards whom you are feeling in any way negative or hostile.

Now settle down into your usual meditation position. Breathe out tension, breathe in feelings of cleansing and relaxation.

Step 2
As your breathing slows down and you become more attuned to its rhythm, feel it as a warming, softening presence in your chest. Let the breath expand and relax the area around your heart. Feel this as a sensation of love, that you are sending to yourself. It may help to recall a particular moment when you have felt especially good. You do not need to recall the particular circumstances, simply to allow the positive feeling about yourself, which you connect with, to expand from your heart outwards. You are sending feelings of loving kindness to yourself.

Step 3
Now bring the person for whom you have loving feelings into your meditation. You do not have to have a mental picture of them, but simply to allow the feelings of love to extend to them from this warm place you have connected to around your heart. Carry on breathing gently in and out, keeping the focus of attention on the breath around the heart area.

Step 4
Extend these feelings of love and warmth to the 'neutral' person you identified. You have generated such positive feelings through your gentle breathing and good intention. Let this flow outwards towards this person too.

Step 5
Allow the person you have difficulty with to enter this heart space. This of course will be the most difficult. We all hang on to reasons for justifying our dislike and antagonism towards others, especially if we feel they have done us wrong in some way. Tell your mind that it can put away the pros and cons of the situation just for the moment, and allow the heart and the breathing to take over. Stay in touch with the feelings of warmth and love you had in the other sections, and allow this to extend now to this person too.

Step 6
Staying close to the breath, allowing any tension to be released, include the whole world within your feelings of loving kindness. You might picture the Earth as though seen spinning through space, and send your feelings directly to it, or you may more generally direct this loving space outwards from you.

Step 7

Withdraw your attention inside yourself again. Feel the breath very gentle in your chest. Notice the feeling of warmth around the heart area. Do you feel different from when you began the meditation? Come out of the meditation very gently; you have touched on a lot of feelings and may be in a particularly delicate state. As with other meditations, it is a good idea to bring yourself back to everyday reality by looking around the room as though to see it for the first time, and gently moving and stretching the body.

Practising metta bhavana

Metta bhavana may sound like a rather wishful thinking bit of do-goodery. There is a lot more to it than that. It has been practised for thousands of years because it integrates mind, feelings and spirit. It is not always easy to extend loving feelings to oneself, let alone someone who might be seen as an enemy. You are not necessarily excusing what they have done, but you are dealing with the feelings you have about them, which can only help both you and the situation. You are also acknowledging that however badly you feel towards them, they too are only human. And you are building up a relaxed and loving attitude to yourself and to the way in which you live in the world.

Atisha's meditation

This meditation has some similarities to the last one which focused on developing loving kindness. Atisha's meditation has a surprising twist to it. You breathe *in* negative thoughts, pain and hurt, and then breathe *out* loving, peaceful thoughts. Atisha was a Tibetan master of meditation, and he recognised that a remarkable alchemy takes place within the body in this process. It's like turning base metal into gold – a transformation takes place within the heart, and negativity is transformed into positivity.

Step 1

Focus on your breathing, letting it become deep and slow. Bring your attention to the breath in the chest area, around the heart. Then as you breathe in, feel as though you are breathing in all the pains and troubles of the world. It might be to do with, perhaps, a hurtful thing that has happened to you personally, or simply the sufferings of the world.

Step 2

Now with every breath out, imagine you are breathing out bliss and happiness. Again focus your attention on the area around the heart, and feel the emotion flowing out from there. The misery that you breathed in is miraculously transformed into joy. Let this pour from you with every out-breath.

Practising Atisha's meditation
This simple method can be a revelation. It enables you to:

● choose joy in preference to sorrow

● deal with hurtful and painful events in a calm way

● be in charge of your own feelings

● contact the part of yourself which can rise easily above difficulties

● create good relationships with others.

It is not surprising that this meditation has been called the way of compassion. As you come to acknowledge your own painful feelings, and to release them, your compassion for others increases of its own accord.

Zazen meditation
This is an unusual meditation in that it is practised with the eyes open. **Zazen** means simply 'sitting meditation' and is one of the traditional practices of Buddhist monks. Having the eyes open is obviously a good way of helping you stay awake if, like these monks, you are spending many hours in meditation. However, helping you to stay awake is far from being the only benefit of this practice. In zazen you will be:

● starting to incorporate your more inwardly turned meditation into contact with the outside world

● finding a balance, a poise, between your inner sensations and external reality

● learning to maintain the awareness you are finding through meditation when faced with distractions from outside.

Zen masters say that in zazen you 'take aim without having a target'. This paradox is typical of Zen teaching, and refers to a state of passive awareness. It is this calm yet alert state that zazen is excellent at encouraging.

Stage 1
Find a place to sit where you can look at something which has few distractions. You may choose simply a blank wall, or perhaps a more

beautiful place such as a view into a garden. Whatever it is, make sure it is somewhere where there is likely to be very little movement to distract you. Some practitioners recommend sitting actually within arm's length of a plain wall.

Stage 2
Sit in whatever meditation position you find most comfortable and in which the back is straight. Have your hands resting on your lap, resting one hand inside the other so that the thumbs touch and make an oval shape. Take a few deep breaths to settle down, and then let your breath settle into a relaxed and easy rhythm for the rest of the meditation.

Stage 3
Keep your eyes half-open throughout the meditation. Look straight ahead of you, but without staring. Let the eyes become soft. You are seeing what is in front of you but not reacting to it in any way, so your vision is relaxed and diffused. If you need to blink, do so, but otherwise try not to move your eyes.

Stage 4
Sit like this for half an hour. Keep your eyes open and as still as possible, also keeping your body immobile. Keep your attention on whatever is happening, moment to moment. Relax but stay aware of bodily sensations, trains of thought and whatever your awareness brings to you.

Practising zazen
This meditation may seem strange initially, but you will soon get the hang of it if you practise it for a while. Try doing it over the course of a week to get an idea of what it offers. It becomes a very enjoyable, intriguing way of letting more and more layers of the mind's stresses drop away.

A Zen master once said, 'While you are doing zazen neither despise nor cherish the thoughts that arise; only search your own mind or heart for the very source of these thoughts.'

QUESTIONS AND ANSWERS

How do I know when I'm witnessing something in meditation?
You will have a sense of seeing what you are thinking or experiencing as though part of you is 'sitting on your own shoulder'. You might, for

instance, drift off into a long train of thought, and then suddenly become aware of these thoughts even as they are still carrying on. That is the moment of witnessing.

I don't quite understand where my attention should be in zazen meditation – in the eyes, in what I'm looking at, or in my breathing?
All and none of these! Your attention in zazen is much more diffused than in many other meditations which have a focal point. Try to allow your awareness to be very general, but to stay sharp. Let yourself enter a relaxed yet watchful state. This is a meditation which has particular repercussions in everyday life; by having your eyes open you are starting to integrate your growing inner meditative state with the world in which you live.

SUMMARY

1. Witnessing is at the root of all meditations.

2. There are many ways of using that most fundamental meditating tool – the breath – as a way of holding the attention.

A Zen master, Shen-hui, said, 'Seeing into nothingness, this is true seeing and eternal seeing.'

5

Trying More Meditations

The whole of life is like playing a game of hide and seek in which you must find your Real Self.

Meher Baba

GAZING MEDITATIONS

Gazing, or **tratak**, is another ancient meditation, and one which can be adapted to all sorts of circumstances. It is a tried and tested way of focusing your attention. Just as in the breathing meditation you use breath as a point to return to whenever possible, in gazing meditations you use an external focus.

In Buddhism the focus for attention has often been a statue of Buddha, portraying stillness and balance. Many other things can be used as the focus for the gaze, such as:

- a candle (see page 64)

- a beautiful object such as a flower

- a picture of a spiritual or religious teacher

- a crystal.

One of the most effective ones is gazing at yourself. This meditation is outlined below.

Self-gazing meditation
You may think you are completely familiar with your face. You probably look at yourself several times a day in the mirror, so how could gazing at yourself possibly be a meditation? Self-gazing is about going beyond the way that you normally see yourself, and can be a profound experience.

Step 1
Set up a mirror in a place where you can sit comfortably while looking

into it. Look at yourself as though you have never seen yourself before, and without passing any judgements about your looks.

Step 2
After a few minutes, gaze just into your own eyes in the mirror. Keep your eyes fixed there, and do not blink. Your eyes may smart and run a bit, and you will eventually have to blink a bit, but try not to for as long as possible. Notice what happens to your face – does it seem to change shape, perhaps to be as though you have never seen yourself, or to take on all sorts of new aspects? Maintain the gazing for about 15 minutes.

You may find that you have some unusual sensations, perhaps that your face almost seems to disappear at times.

Step 3
Close your eyes, and take your attention within yourself. Notice how you feel about the way you saw yourself. You may notice new sensations, a feeling of having gone beyond your normal reality as you contacted a part of yourself that is beyond the way we normally identify ourselves. Stay in touch with any strong, inner sensations which you now know are within you and not dependent on your physical body or perceptions. Slowly move into relaxing into your breathing, for about 30 or 45 minutes.

Practising self-gazing
This meditation is sometimes done over an extended period of time, such as once a day for a month, in order for the experience of the self to be fully explored. Trying it even once, though, is an unforgettable experience.

Mandala meditation
A **mandala** is a diagram or picture which is used as the focal point for a gazing meditation. The picture always has a central point, and is usually contained within a circle. Sometimes the shapes are purely abstract patterns; in Tibetan Tantric Buddhism elaborate images of gods and people may also appear. A square is sometimes included within the circle, signifying the earth within the universe. The mandala represents ideas like wholeness, perfection, the absolute, cosmic consciousness, and provides the meditator with a way of contacting this within themselves. A simple example is shown in Figure 5.

Some mandalas are wonderfully rich and elaborate, containing a wealth of symbolism. The colours used in them also have their own meanings, such as sky-blue representing the eternal, yellow for spiritual growth, red for devotion, and gold for spiritual wealth.

Step 1
Place a mandala such as the one in this book in front of you, at eye level. It should be at a distance where your eyes can move easily over the whole area of the pattern.

Step 2
Sitting still, allow your breath to deepen and your face to relax, especially the muscles around the eyes. Let your eyes be soft. Now look at the centre of the mandala, then move your eyes slowly to the edge of it. Let all thoughts go, just taking in the pattern. Take your gaze back in towards the centre.

Step 3
Close your eyes. Then repeat the gazing, moving slowly from the centre to the outside and back again a few times. You will probably find that your gaze is increasingly drawn to the centre. Let it rest there more and more.

Fig. 5. A mandala for meditation.

Step 4
Close your eyes. Sit quietly for a while, looking at any after-image of
the mandala that remains.

LOOKING AT TRANSCENDENTAL MEDITATION

Transcendental meditation, or TM, became well known in the West in
the 1960s. It could be said to have made meditation a household word
when the Beatles famously learned about it in 1967, and researchers
started studying its effects in 1968. It was introduced to the USA in 1959
by Maharishi Mahesh Yogi, and at one time 'meditation' and
'transcendental meditation' were virtually synonymous, as few people
outside religious communities were meditating before then. Now more
than 1.5 million Americans have taken TM classes.

Practitioners claim that if just one per cent of the population took it
up, society would be transformed and, in particular, be much less
stressful. A large part of the research into meditation – some 500
scientific studies – has been based on TM.

Practising TM

TM is based in part on Hindu meditation. Meditators are given a mantra
(a special word or phrase – see below) which they silently repeat many
times. This mantra is never to be told to anyone else, or written down.
TM is always taught by a teacher, so a certain amount of secrecy
surrounds it.

For details of where to learn TM, see Useful Addresses.

USING SOUND

Working with mantras

A mantra is a word or phrase that is repeated over and over again, as an
aid to meditation. The original meaning of the word translates as
something like 'a tool (*tra*) for thought (*man*)'.

The use of mantras is literally thousands of years old. Their first
known use was even before Hinduism was founded, around 4,000 years
ago in India. Opinion has always been divided about whether the word
used should have a meaning, or whether the meaning is irrelevant and
it's the repetition that is important. Certainly it does appear that the
repetition itself sets up a slightly auto-hypnotic state, in which
meditation may be more accessible.

Although mantras are usually associated with Hinduism and Buddhism, similar practices are found in other religions too. Islam, for instance, has similar practices. Christianity also makes use of repeated incantations, as in the *Hail Mary*, the *Apostles' Creed*, or *Kyrie Eleison Christe Eleison*. The same basic principle applies as when the mantra is *Ram* or *Om* (two frequently used mantras). According to **neuro linguistic programming (NLP)** the repetition of a word programmes the body's neurones, and this is also thought to be what happens with **affirmations**.

Meditating with a mantra

Step 1
Choose your mantra. It may be completely meaningless, just a word whose sound you enjoy and which touches you in some way, or it may have a particular meaning for you, such as 'peace' or 'love'. You may prefer to choose a mantra that has been practised through the ages, such as one of the following:

- *Om* (pronounced ohm). This is considered to be the mantra of all mantras, the sound of the universe itself.

- *Ram* (pronounced rahm). An Indian mantra to promote truth and virtue.

- *Sita* (pronounced see-tah). The female counterpart to Ram; when the two are put together to make the mantra *Sitaram*, the balance of male/female is complete.

- *Om Mani Padme Hum.* Means 'om, the jewel in the lotus' and is said to develop compassion and spirituality.

- *Hare Krishna.* Used particularly by followers of the Krishna Consciousness Movement, as a means of religious devotion.

- *Peace.*

- *Love.*

- *Lord Jesus Christ, have mercy on me.* Used in the Christian tradition in a similar way to a mantra.

- *La ilaha illa'llah* (there is no God but God). A Sufi form of mantra, known in the Islamic tradition as a **dhikr**. A dhikr, it is said, should be recited with 'the tongue of the heart'.

- *Soham* (pronounced soh-hum). Another Indian mantra, meaning 'I am that' and aiming to unite the meditator with the absolute.

Step 2
Sitting comfortably, repeat your chosen mantra either aloud, very quietly or silently in your mind. Set your own pace, experimenting as to whether you prefer to do it very rapidly or slowly.

Feel the mantra vibrating all over your body, as though it is music. Notice when it becomes automatic and other thoughts have intruded, and bring your attention back to the mantra.

Practising using a mantra
Try using your mantra for several days in order to judge the effect it is having. Preferably do it several times a day. Some critics of using mantras say it tends to put you to sleep rather than make you more conscious. See what you think.

Humming

This may not sound like a meditation technique, but it is actually an ancient Tibetan method. Traditionally it would have been done by monks in the early hours of the morning. As our lives are rather different from those of Tibetan monks, try it at any time of day. Humming is a wonderful way to:

● still the mind

● produce a soothing vibration that relaxes body and emotions

● focus the attention within yourself.

It also, according to Tibetan custom, has a healing effect on the organs of the body.

Everyone knows how to hum. When you use it as a meditation you are just tuning into something that you have probably done since childhood.

Step 1
Sit in a comfortable position. Allow your breath to settle down. Keeping your mouth closed, and breathing in and out through your nose, start to hum. Let it be a continuous note rather than a tune.

Step 2
Continue humming for between 30 and 45 minutes. You can vary the note up or down as you feel inclined. Hum as loudly or as quietly as you feel inclined. Keep your attention on the gentle vibration that is produced within the body.

Step 3
Stop humming. Allow yourself at least 15 minutes to sit quietly, staying in tune with the vibrant stillness you will have produced.

Practising humming
There is a further, more elaborate meditation based on humming, called **nadabrahma.** This will take you more deeply into this lovely technique (see page 69 for details). It can also be done with a partner (see page 102).

Through humming you are creating a kind of inner music or harmony. It is an excellent way to harmonise yourself – it has even been claimed as a great aid to dieting, as you become more aware of when your inner harmony has been disturbed by eating too much.

TRYING MORE TECHNIQUES

Darkness meditation
Not for the faint-hearted! On the other hand, meditators do start finding they have inner resources they never dreamt of before.

Darkness meditation is said to have been practised by the Essenes, a pre-Christian spiritual and mystical movement. It is simply a breath meditation, but practised in a place which is as entirely free from light as possible. Some people find that meditating in complete darkness enriches their practice very powerfully; for others it is a way of also confronting some fears about the dark and all it implies, in a safe and ordered way.

If you try this meditation, make sure that you do it:

- in a place that you know to be completely safe and secure

- ideally, at least to begin with, with other people with whom you feel at ease.

Stage 1
The setting up for this meditation is all-important. You are trying to create a place where no light at all – not even a crack – is visible. The ideal place would be somewhere like a cellar or basement, but most people will have to improvise. Choose a room where no light comes in from outside, perhaps with thick curtains. If necessary block out any light coming through cracks in the door. It really does need to be completely lightproof!

Set the cushions or chairs out so that anyone meditating will be as comfortable as possible. You may need to have a torch to hand.

Stage 2
The meditation is done in complete darkness, usually for an hour. If you are doing this with other people, make sure everyone is settled and at ease before one person checks the room for chinks of light. Once the room is totally dark, take time to settle down. Sit with your eyes open for a while, then close your eyes. Feel how the outer darkness is now no different to what it's like when you close your eyes and go within yourself. Take a few deep breaths and notice how you feel about being here.

Stage 3
Meditate on the breath, as in the Basic Meditation (Chapter 2). Does it feel different from when you are meditating in a light room? If you feel any nervousness, try to breathe into it and allow it to pass, just as any other thoughts do, and come back to the breathing.

Stage 4
After an hour, come out of the meditation very slowly so that you can adjust to the lights whilst remaining in your state of increased awareness. Be gentle with yourself for a while, you may feel a little vulnerable.

The respiratory one method
This was developed by Dr Herbert Benson, the Harvard medical professor who led the way in research into meditation. Having pin-pointed the key principles that all meditations have in common, he decided to develop them into his own system. It is very straightforward – really just a variation on the mantra meditations.

Step 1
Sit in a comfortable, relaxed position.

Step 2
Focus on your breath. Mentally repeat the word 'one' each time you breathe out.

WORKING WITH THE CHAKRAS

Science, it seems, is starting to catch up with much of the ancient knowledge that our rational ways of thinking have dismissed. The beneficial effects of meditation have been scientifically tested and proven beyond doubt. And now even some of the more esoteric parts of meditation are starting to gain scientific credibility.

The **chakras** are seven centres of energy located throughout the body. According to ancient Indian lore they represent different types of energy ranging from the physical and earthly through to the most spiritual. They are said to represent the different aspects of our beings that we all possess, and through which we need to progress in order to achieve our highest potential as conscious human beings. Figure 6 shows where the chakras are situated, what attributes they have and what part of our energy system they affect. What is remarkable is that this ancient energy system is now being accredited by discoveries that the chakras do correspond to appropriate endocrine systems and nerve clusters.

Chakra	Position	Colour	Controls	Energetic function
1st	Base of pine	Red	Reproductive organs	Survival, sexuality, physical control
2nd	Between navel and genitals	Orange	Spine, kidneys, adrenals	Emotions, sensuality
3rd	Solar plexus	Yellow	Stomach, muscles, pancreas	Power, self-expression, vitality
4th	Middle of chest	Green	Circulation, heart, immune system, thymus	Love, relating
5th	Throat	Blue	Lungs, bronchial system, metabolism, thyroid	Communication, creativity, authenticity
6th	'Third eye', between eyebrows	Indigo	Lower brain, pituitary	Intuition, inner vision, spiritual awareness
7th	Top of head	Violet	Upper brain, pineal	Universal consciousness

Fig. 6. The chakra system.

Chakra meditation

The aim of meditating on each of the chakras in turn is to activate and energise them. As each chakra is related to particular aspects of life, any difficulties in that area can affect the chakra, and vice versa.

Step 1
You can do this meditation either sitting, lying down or standing up. Allow the breath to settle down.

Step 2
Take your attention to each chakra in turn, working from the lowest up towards the top one. The position of each of the chakras is shown in Figure 6, along with the colour associated with it. So as you bring your attention to the first chakra, which is located in the lower pelvis, imagine the colour red in that area. When you feel you have located and energised that chakra, move up to the second chakra, slightly below the navel, and flood that area with orange in your imagination. Progress up through the chakras in this way until you have reached the chakra inside and above the top of the head.

Step 3
Feel the energy flowing up through you, from the lowest to the highest chakra. If you feel it as vibrant and alive you are experiencing what is known as **kundalini** or serpent power by the Yogis. Enjoy any feelings of being energised and cleansed.

Step 4
An optional extra at the end of a chakra meditation is to feel yourself bathed in pure white light. You are combining all the colours you have experienced. This is a very good healing meditation. Feel the vibrant white light both within and without you, coming into you from the top of your head downwards and washing away any impurities. Let it cleanse and revitalise you.

Working with the chakra meditation
You can work very deeply with the chakras. An elaborate system of sounds, colours, even body postures has been devised to access the chakras (see Figure 6).

QUESTIONS AND ANSWERS

Sometimes my thoughts seem to be all over the place, and for every minute meditating I spend ten minutes thinking and day-dreaming. Is it worth it?

The fact that you have seen how your mind gets distracted is hugely beneficial in itself. Meditation has been likened to going down into the basement to do the filing – when we sit in meditation we become aware of the mind's activity, and it seems to take the opportunity to bring all our current preoccupations to the fore. So this constant mind-activity has some benefit. We can notice it, and then move on from it when we are able to, having 'done the filing'!

I would like to try doing the darkness meditation, but I know I wouldn't be able to completely black out my room. Is there any way round this?

Make the place you are meditating in as dark as possible, and then wear an eye-mask. This can be simply a scarf that you tie loosely around your eyes when you are ready to start the meditation. You may be able to get hold of a specially made eye-mask which will do the job even better, being made of light-proof material with elastic to hold it in place. You could buy or make one, or ask for one to help you sleep next time you travel by air – use it on the plane to try a high-altitude meditation too!

Doing darkness meditation this way may have a slightly different effect, but can still be very profound.

6

Meditating to Reduce Stress

'Be unto yourself a refuge. Strive mindfully.'

The last words of the Buddha

We humans have developed fantastic brains which are constantly monitoring, assimilating and acting on information. Nowadays we are so bombarded with input to the brain that having a way of stepping out of this intense activity is becoming more and more vital, for the sake of our health and well-being.

SOFTENING AND RELAXING

The meditations in this chapter all provide ways of releasing stress. You don't need to wait until you feel stressed to try them, of course. Many of them are also traditional methods which have long been found to enhance calmness, and to help mind and body to soften and relax.

Gibberish meditation

Like a pool being fed by a stream, our brains are being constantly filled up with all the normal things of life. That's fine, unless the thoughts stay there, washing around and having no outlet. It is very useful to have a way of instantly releasing some of these thoughts. This is a way of letting some of the overflow of thoughts spill out.

Gibberish is both a meditation in its own right and an excellent way of beginning any meditation at all. It clears away some of the clutter and opens up a space in the mind – the ultimate cobweb-blower, perhaps. Don't be put off by how bizarre it sounds. You probably will feel quite self-conscious initially, but if you stick with it you will notice an immediate effect. It actually has an ancient pedigree; the Bible refers to people 'talking in tongues' or *glossolalia*. It goes deep into the unconscious mind, and soon becomes flowing and easy to do.

Step 1
Sitting in your normal position for meditation, start talking out loud. Start with something like 'la, la, la,' but then let it go into nonsense, not

recognisable words or phrases. Let your tongue take over, so that all sorts of gibberish come out. It's rather like being a baby again, using the voice to make sounds with no apparent meaning. Let it be as though you are talking in a strange language whose words you know well but whose meaning is irrelevant.

Step 2
Let your body come into this releasing activity now. Stay seated, but move your arms, head and shoulders in a way that feels in tune with the gibberish, such as a shaking movement. Be lively and dynamic about it. Move the muscles of the face into all sorts of odd shapes and stretches as you gibber. Go more deeply into the gibberish, bringing all your attention to the strange 'words' and starting to drop your self-consciousness.

Step 3
Stop. Be absolutely still. These moments of emptiness are precious. Attune to them, and to your inner stillness.

Timing
Gibberish meditation can be used in various different ways, so the length of time for which you should do it will also vary. It can be used for:

- A whole meditation in its own right, for half an hour. Do the gibberish for 15 minutes, then lie on your stomach for 15 minutes, absolutely still and in contact with the earth and with the empty space within yourself.

- A 'cleanser' prior to other meditations, for about five minutes.

- A way of stilling the mind before sleep. Do the gibberish for 15 minutes, sitting upright in bed, then just lie down and sleep. If you practise this over a period of time your sleep will deepen and bring you a new freshness.

- A week's meditation by itself, prior to moving into another meditation. An excellent way of preparing yourself for embarking on a sustained period of practising meditation.

RELEASING STRESS THROUGH MEDITATION

Many of the meditations outlined in the next chapter on active meditations are good ways of reducing stress, as they use physical activity. But you can also release stress in more gentle ways. The following meditations are simple techniques which will leave you feeling inwardly calm.

Candle-gazing

If you have already tried the self-gazing meditation (page 51) you will have experienced the power of a gazing meditation. Candle-gazing is much softer than self-gazing, and is an excellent stress-releaser. This is another good meditation for beginners.

Step 1
Set up a candle in a draught-free room, ideally so that it is at your eye level when you are sitting in your meditation position. It should be close enough that you can stare deep into the flame without straining your eyes or neck muscles.

Sit down in front of the candle. Take a few minutes to let your breath slow down and to move into a more relaxed state.

When you feel ready start gazing at the candle flame. Let your eyes be soft; although you are looking at the flame, your sight should be unfocused so that you are not staring intently at the flame but letting it gently fill your vision. Keep your eyes on the flame, do not allow them to wander off elsewhere.

Step 2
After five or ten minutes of gazing at the candle, close your eyes. You will probably see an after-image of the flame. Make this the focus of your attention now, seeing the intense glow of the colours. Feel as though this is slowly expanding to fill the whole of your body.

Step 3
Gaze at the flame again, increasingly feeling at one with it, as though your body and the flame are melting into each other.

Step 4
Continue alternating candle-gazing and sitting with eyes closed. Finish the meditation with an extended period of closed-eyes' meditation.

Expanding on candle-gazing meditation
This same technique can be used on any object that you find inspiring, although the light of a candle does have a particularly soothing effect.

You can take this practice further by trying the next meditation, which combines breathing with candle-gazing.

Breathing and gazing
A lovely meditation which will leave you feeling both energised and calm. This hour-long meditation combines the technique of candle-gazing with breathing and gentle body movements. Accompany your meditation with flowing music if you like. Have a lit candle set up near you before you start the meditation, so that you do not have to stop between any of the stages.

Step 1
Sit with closed eyes. Breathe in deeply through the nose, holding the breath for as long as possible. Breathe out gently through the mouth, keeping the lungs empty for as long as you can manage. Continue this breathing cycle for 15 minutes, making the breaths quite forceful.

Step 2
Go back to normal breathing, open your eyes and gaze at the candle flame. Let your gaze be soft. 15 minutes.

Step 3
Keeping your eyes closed, stand up. Staying in touch with the subtle energies that have built up in you during the first two stages, allow your body to gently move and sway. The movement is very natural and flowing, not controlled as in a dance. Take it very gently, allowing graceful movements to come of their own accord. 15 minutes.

Step 4
Lie down on the floor for a further 15 minutes. Keep your eyes closed, enjoy the sense of stillness.

Listening
This is a meditation which can be done either in your usual meditation space, or even when you are out and about in the world. It is a good way of disconnecting from the busy-ness with which we are usually surrounded, whilst staying within the everyday world which we have to live in.

Step 1
Sit with your eyes closed, allowing your breath to slow and deepen.

Step 2
Take your attention to your hearing. Notice what noises are going on, close to you or in the far distance. Gradually let the noises become like

a piece of music; you are just listening, not getting involved with them. Maybe you hear the sound of a TV in the background – let it just be there rather than trying to hear what's being said. Or perhaps you hear the noise of a siren in the distance and find your mind speculating on what's happening. Bring it back to hearing just a symphony of noise.

Step 3
Return to your breathing whenever you notice that you have got hooked into involvement with one particular noise. Then return to listening again, allowing the sounds around you to become more and more soothing, as though they are part of you. Finish whenever you feel ready.

Practising listening
This can be a useful meditation for:

● When you are meditating at home and there are other people also using the house.

● When you are out in the world, and need to recharge yourself and find some inner calm. Try doing it when you are sitting in a café, for instance, or waiting in a car, or even in a stressful situation such as being in a hospital.

The main thing is to remain passive. You are not judging what you hear, but simply enjoying the connection that happens through listening between the outside world and your inner being.

Listening to silence
It may sound like a contradiction to suggest that you listen to silence. Yet silence has a richness, a depth and is something that is as precious as it is rare today. When you do have the opportunity to 'listen to the silence', allow your own inner silence which arises through meditation to become one with the silence around you.

Listening to music and other sounds
Just as you can use any object for a gazing meditation, you can use any sound as a means of focusing your attention in meditation.

Music
Music is all around us, on the radio, TV, in the shops and playing from the ice-cream van. In this meditation it is important to listen to the music, rather than letting it be there as background noise. Choose music that is soothing and has some depth to it. Heavy metal, for instance

would not be a good choice. Western and Eastern classical music can be used, or some of the 'new age' tapes are good.

Because we're so familiar with hearing music, it's tempting to treat this meditation in a different way from others. But if it is approached with the same commitment and intention, this can be an excellent way of touching inner calm. Listening to music has been shown to make changes in the body which are connected with relaxation.

Prepare yourself for your meditation in the usual way, then hear the music as though it is being played inside you. Each time your thoughts stray, bring them back to the music. Listen to the silences between the notes, too. It is like the deep, expectant pause that happens between breathing in and breathing out.

Other sounds

Have you ever felt mesmerised by the sound of train wheels clacking over the railway tracks? Listening to the rhythm they set up seems to induce a state rather like repeating a mantra. Make use of any such man-made noise, such as the ticking of a clock or watch. Let the sound be the focus of your meditation.

Ancient Yoga writings suggest meditating near water: waterfalls, rushing rivers, the patter of rain, a splashing fountain, the gentle lapping of a lake all provide a focus. The sound of the sea rhythmically washing across the sand or sucking at the pebbles is wonderfully releasing. These kinds of natural sounds also connect the meditator with nature and have the added bonus of exposure to air containing negative ions, which induce clarity of mind. Follow the simple basic rules: sitting still, breathing gently and listening to the sound with passive awareness.

LETTING GO OF ANXIETY

Anxiety/bliss meditation

In this meditation you bring any difficult feelings to the forefront of your attention – and then breathe them away.

Step 1

Take your time preparing for this meditation, by perhaps setting out some flowers or a candle to honour your intention of releasing your anxieties. Have some fresh air coming into the room.

When you have settled into your meditation position, let your breath get slower and slower. Spend some time over this, so that you have gone quite deeply into connecting with your breath before you start Step 2.

Step 2
Let your breath become very strong and deep. It should feel as though you are filling and emptying your lungs as fully as possible. Do this for a few breaths. Then with your next breath out get a mental picture of the breath coming out of your body and looking like deep, dark maroon smoke. Imagine all the things that are troubling you leaving your body along with this breath. Feel it as a strong force, and allow the emotion of your anger, fear, stress or whatever it is to be expelled with this maroon-coloured breath.

Step 3
With the next breath in, breathe in golden light. Imagine all the things you would prefer to feel – maybe peace, calm, joy, acceptance – coming in with the breath. As with the maroon breath out, try to feel the golden light as a strong physical force coming in with your deep inhalation. Let it flood through you.

Step 4
Alternate between the two breaths for about five minutes or until you feel that some release has happened within you. Return to normal deep breathing for a while. You might finish the meditation by placing your hands in a prayer position, or over your heart, and acknowledging your courage and openness.

CULTIVATING INNER CALM

You have started ridding yourself of stress and anxiety through meditation by trying some of the meditations above. Some of the more physical ones in the next chapter are also excellent stress-busters. As your anxiety levels drop you may become more aware of a silent, peaceful place within yourself There are many meditations which enhance this state of calm, and the more you use them the less likely you are to be prone to stress in the first place.

They are also very enjoyable. Try doing the second stage of the breathing and gazing meditation above (page 65) on its own, for instance. By just allowing the body to move slowly and spontaneously you can move easily into a state of calm. Follow the movement with a time of sitting, so that you can attune to this state of ease which is your natural self.

Nadabrahma, or humming meditation

Humming meditation (nadabrahma) is an ancient Tibetan method. The vibration of the humming has a soothing effect on body and mind, opening the way to a sense of clarity and peace. It is done for an hour.

Step 1
Sit with closed eyes. Keeping your lips together, start humming. It can be loud enough for anyone nearby to hear you, but do not strain yourself. Feel the hum coming from low in your abdomen, and allow the note to vary if you like. You can also slowly move your body if you wish to. 30 minutes.

Step 2
Hold your hands palms upwards at navel level. Very slowly move them forwards together, then divide the hands and make two large circles left and right until the hands return to the navel. Imagine energy and love flowing from your hands out to the universe. Repeat this very slow circling movement for seven-and-a-half minutes. Now turn the hands so that the palms face downwards, still at navel level. Start moving them in the opposite direction from the first circles, so that they are moving in towards you. Imagine energy flowing in to you; do this also for seven-and-a-half minutes.

Step 3
Lie down. Keep your eyes closed, staying absolutely still for 15 minutes.

Practising nadabrahma
Humming meditation has been made more accessible to the West by the spiritual teacher Osho. Special music has been composed which makes it much easier to attune to each section – and so that you don't need to clock-watch. See Useful Addresses.

Osho also suggested a variation on nadabrahima for couples, which is described in Chapter 10.

Connecting meditation

We are rooted in the earth, made of very physical material, but we are also connected with the universe through thoughts, feelings and spirit. This meditation brings those different elements together, uniting them within you. This meditation can take as long as you like – a few minutes or an hour. Although it can be done at any time of day it is particularly powerful when done just before going to bed.

Step 1
Kneel on the floor, with eyes closed. Inhale, raise your arms high in the air, fingers reaching up. Imagine you are drawing the energy of the universe down into your fingertips and into your body. You might experience this energy as light, as love, or however it feels to you.

Step 2
Breathe out, and lower your arms and body to the floor so that your forehead and hands rest on the ground. Breathe into the earth, feeling your connection with the ground.

Step 3
Repeat this cycle several times, becoming aware of the connection between heaven and earth, sky and ground, passing through your body.

Step 4
Lie on your back with your eyes closed for a few minutes. Appreciate the richness of the connections you have made within yourself.

Meditating on a flower
As well as beautifying your meditation space with flowers, you can use them for meditations.

● Walking past a flower, inhale its perfume in the split second before your mind comes in and starts saying how beautiful it is, or that you prefer other colours or any such judgements. In that split second you can become as one with the flower.

● Use a single bloom as the focus for a gazing meditation, as you would a candle.

● To meditate on the transience of life, choose a flower such as a rose that will last for several days. Spend ten minutes a day for a week gazing at it, getting to know it and noticing the changes that happen to it from day to day. Acknowledge any feelings you have about these changes, and how they relate to your own life, and then return to just gazing at the flower in passive appreciation.

'Stop' meditation
Gurdjieff, a 20th century Armenian teacher, used a technique to bring his pupils' attention and awareness back to the present moment. He would suddenly shout 'stop' while they were in the middle of some activity, such as working or eating. They would have to stay frozen in

that position for quite some time, so that they could reconnect with their inner selves. The aim of this was to encourage greater awareness in everyday activities.

You may not have anyone to shout 'stop' at you as you are walking down the street, but you can adapt the method. You can instantly freeze in position and bring your attention back inside yourself. Set yourself a goal of doing this six times a day for a week. You could even set an alarm clock to give a wake-up-to-yourself call.

USING MEDITATION TO HELP REST AND SLEEP

Just as you will find that meditation makes you less likely to get drawn into arguments, to dwell on difficult situations or to get things out of perspective, so you will almost certainly find that practising meditation has a beneficial effect on your sleep.

If you do have existing sleep problems, though, you might like to try some meditative methods for improving things.

Unravelling the day
This was originally a Sufi meditation. It is an excellent way of putting the day in perspective, letting it go and moving into a more restful state. It can be done either as a sitting meditation or when you are already in bed.

Stage 1
Make yourself comfortable. Imagine the day you have just experienced as though it is a ball of wool. See the end of the wool poking out, and imagine this to be the most recent thing that happened to you.

Stage 2
Now start 'unravelling' the day, as though you are slowly teasing out the wool, pulling the thread out so that the ball of wool unwinds. Go back slowly through the day, recalling events from now backwards. Try to recall:

● what happened at a particular time

● what the scene looked like, what was around you

● how this event made you feel at the time.

If you notice that you are getting caught up in the event, just re-live it a little longer and then move on from it. You will be most likely to get caught up in the events that created strong feelings for you, and these are the very ones that are most likely to impair your sleep. Don't brush them to one side, look at them as dispassionately as you can and then move back to the previous event.

Stage 3
You will probably fall asleep before you get back to the start of the day. Excellent. If not, and you find that you have reached back to when you awoke this morning, see the whole of the ball of wool – the day – drifting off. Come back to your breathing and assure yourself that you can now relax.

Positive memories meditation
Another meditation which helps set the day's events in context. Useful to sound sleepers and insomniacs alike.

When you are lying in bed, recall six positive things that happened to you during the day. Not every day is going to have some unusually good event in it, for which you might open up the champagne. The point of this meditation is to remember the 'ordinary' things that can be overlooked but which have added to the joy of the day. It could be something like the taste of some good food, the sight of a bird flying, relaxing in the bath … anything which just made you feel good to be alive.

Sleep-awareness meditation
It has been said that if you can stay in a state of awareness even when asleep, then meditation is really going deep. For most of us this is probably only something we can understand in theory, but it is possible to get a glimpse of this state, where meditation has become integrated into life.

Technique 1
As you are going to sleep, try to maintain your consciousness of what is happening. Don't fight the sleep, but stay aware as long as possible of your body relaxing and your mind becoming slower. Notice how the awareness is different from the thoughts in your mind.

Technique 2
As you are waking up become aware of yourself without bringing yourself to full wakefulness. Stay aware of this point where you are neither asleep nor awake, but balanced between the two. You may find

that dreams resurface at this time; again, see if you can maintain your awareness if this happens, and not fall asleep again.

Technique 3
Have you ever had a dream where you know that you are dreaming, but don't wake, and perhaps have some conscious control over what happens in the dream? This is called **conscious dreaming**. Through meditating you may find that these kinds of dreams happen more, of their own accord. You can also try cultivating this ability, as a way of exploring aspects of the dream-world you would like to work with.

As you are going to sleep, and very nearly in sleep, tell yourself that you will be aware of your dreams. Give yourself a strong message that you repeat a few times. Allow time in the morning to recall what happened. It may take a while to get in touch with your dreams in this way, but it can be a useful part of your journey into your inner being.

Golden light meditation
This is a meditation to do either just before sleeping or first thing in the morning, the very moment you wake up.

Step 1
Do this just as you start coming out of sleep, or when you are relaxing before sleeping and are neither quite awake nor asleep. Keeping your eyes closed, breathe in, and picture a golden light coming into your head and flooding down through your body. Feel this strong light like the rising sun, passing right down through you from the top of your head and out through your toes, as though your body is hollow.

Step 2
Breathe out, and as you do so imagine darkness coming in through your toes and washing up through your body like a great river, leaving through the top of the head. This is a soothing, calming energy that cleanses and refreshes. Keeping the breath slow, alternate between the two breaths, the golden light followed by the dark river. Do the whole meditation for about 20 minutes. Don't worry if you fall asleep while doing it at night – this is actually beneficial as it will carry on working in the subconscious.

Practising golden light meditation
This simple meditation is said to move your energy from the lowest sex centre to the highest spiritual one, when practised over time.

QUESTIONS AND ANSWERS

I feel I might be too tense to even be able to do some of these stress-reducing meditations!
Recognising that you are tense is the first step, which you have taken. You might find the gibberish meditation especially useful before going into anything else. You can also try some of the meditations in the next chapter which release physical tension too. You may find, though, that now that you have acknowledged the tension you can slowly allow yourself to ease down a bit, with meditations like candle-gazing and humming.

Wouldn't having a good night's sleep be just as beneficial as doing a meditation?
Research has shown that stress, as manifested in the body, is not necessarily reduced by sleep. Stress-related hormones measured in the urine have been found to be as high after sleep as before. The same tests have shown that meditation, on the other hand, can reduce stress and affect the physical symptoms it produces. You will also find that meditation does in any case have a beneficial affect on how well you sleep.

SUMMARY

1. Try out several different stress-reducing meditations to see which you find the easiest to use. Then work with this one for an extended period such as 28 days.

2. Meditation brings about a profound inner calm by bringing your attention to that deep, unchanging part of yourself which *is* always at peace.

7

Using Active Meditations

Meditation is neither a journey in space nor a journey in time, but an instantaneous awakening.

J. Krishnamurti

Meditation is usually thought of as something that is done sitting quietly and in stillness. Meditation developed at a time when most people would have been engaged in physically demanding work, and sitting still would have been an important part of the process of finding inner peace. Nowadays, though, many of us get little more exercise than walking between the front door and the car. Because we live such sedentary lives, we tend to carry a lot of tension within our bodies. So it is not surprising that in recent times some new approaches to meditation have been found – through the body. These approaches to meditation may:

● use physical movement, such as dancing, as a meditation in its own right, or

● start with some kind of physical movement as a way of releasing stress, before going on to a still meditation, or

● use some form of everyday physical activity as a focus for meditation.

This chapter gives you meditations to tap into the energy and delight of the physical body.

RAISING YOUR ENERGY LEVELS

The two meditations in this section are very different ways of raising your energy levels. The lotus meditation is very slow and gentle, encouraging a gradual lightening. The dancing meditation is perhaps a more familiar way of raising energy, through the charge you can feel from dancing intently.

Lotus meditation

A traditional Yoga meditation.

Step 1
Stand upright, feet together and arms by your side. Close your eyes and feel your feet planted firmly on the floor. Take a few minutes to let your breath deepen, and feel your body lengthening upwards, almost of its own accord.

Step 2
Imagine that just in front of you on the ground is a beautiful lotus flower. See the colours in it glowing. Now bend from the waist towards this imaginary flower. Cup your hands around it, and straighten up so slowly that the movement is barely perceptible. As you do so, imagine the lotus is lighting up each part of your body as it passes by, both inside and out. So as you reach towards the top of the head your body is aglow with light, within and without. Raise your arms above your head and release the imagined lotus.

Step 3
Repeat the process, but this time imagine the lotus to be slightly to the right of you. You bend from the waist down towards it, and raise it through the right-hand side of your body.

Step 4
As Step 3, but to the left. Then return to your upright standing position and feel the energy rising up through your body, which is now aglow. You may wish to finish by lying on the ground for a while.

Practising the lotus meditation
This is an excellent energy-raiser if you are feeling jaded. The lotus is traditionally a symbol of what can happen through the practice of meditation, an exquisite flower which grows from the mud.

> *In your body is the garden of flowers.*
> *Take your seat on the thousand petals of the lotus,*
> *and there gaze on the Infinite Beauty.*
>
> Kabir

Dancing into meditation

You may have already had a taste of meditation without realising it.

Have you ever danced and danced, becoming as one with the dance? You may have been experiencing the increase in the brain's alpha waves which are connected with meditation. To reach this, though, dancing has to be more than a social event – it has to be a turning inside, becoming the dance itself as much as being the dancer.

Step 1
Choose some music with a fast rhythm, ideally which gradually builds up the tempo. Wear loose, comfortable clothes and move the furniture back! Take a few minutes to ground yourself before putting on the music – breathe, feel your feet on the floor, start moving your body a little. Then put the music on, close your eyes and immerse yourself in the dance. Bring your mind back to your moving body whenever you notice it has wandered. Be passionate about the dancing. Dance for about 30 minutes, or as long as the music lasts, keeping your eyes closed throughout.

Step 2
As soon as the music stops, lie down on the floor on your back. Keep your eyes closed, feel the energy that you have built up through your dancing. Enjoy the sensation, allow your breathing to slow down, and melt into the floor beneath you and the air above. This section is as important as the first, as you are consciously getting to know your own energy.

MOVING INTO STILLNESS

By using the body in certain ways it is possible to enter more easily into the part of ourselves which *is* always calm and still. Sometimes that feels a million miles away, but these meditations provide a reminder that it never really goes away. As a sage once said, 'The mirror of your being is always there… it just needs a little cleaning from time to time.'

Kundalini
The Indian spiritual teacher Osho devised this meditation specifically for Westerners. He said we are too caught up in the mind's preoccupations to be able to drop easily into meditation, and suggested some wonderful ways of quietening body and mind prior to stiller meditation. However, the whole sequence should be regarded as a meditation, which is what makes it different from just taking exercise – your intention to remain aware, to be a witness, is all-important.

It is possible to do this meditation to any music (lively for the first two steps, soft for the third, none for the fourth), but some specially produced music is helpful, available from Osho Purnima (see Useful Addresses).

Step 1
Standing with your eyes either open or closed, be loose and let your whole body shake. Feel the energy moving up from your feet. Allow the shaking to move throughout your body, finding more and more muscles to shake and release. Let go of control, so that the body and the shaking become one. 15 minutes.

Step 2
Dance, in whatever way you feel. Let the whole body enter in, moving as you choose and keeping your awareness in the free movement. 15 minutes.

Step 3
Either sit down or remain standing but still. Close your eyes, witnessing whatever is happening inside and outside you. 15 minutes.

Step 4
Keeping your eyes closed, lie down. Be still. Let your awareness go to your breath or wherever it chooses, but stay attuned to whatever is happening. 15 minutes.

Whirling

Once you have tried this extraordinary meditation, you will understand why the whirling dervishes are so well known. It is not just that whirling looks so spectacular, it is also one of the great meditations.

Prepare for the meditation by arranging a large empty space, perhaps with a few cushions around the edges. It is advisable not to eat for three hours before whirling. Wear loose, flowing clothes. Traditionally a very full-skirted robe is worn which adds to the spinning movement. You also need some really good, lively music – something Eastern is particularly appropriate.

Remember twirling when you were a child... connect with the whirling planet... and away you go.

Step 1
Stand upright. Cross your arms over your chest so that your palms rest

on the opposite shoulder. Keep your eyes open throughout the meditation, until the resting stage.

Step 2
Raise your right hand and arm in the air, loosely pointing upwards. Hold your left arm at shoulder height, the palm facing downwards. Start to turn in an anti-clockwise direction. Use the left foot as an anchor, so that you are whirling on the spot.

Step 3
Take time to build up the speed, depending on how long you are going to whirl for. It is sometimes done for hours on end, but even ten minutes is a real experience. Go faster and faster, all the time watching your surroundings spin around you. Try to stay more in touch with the stillness at the centre of your being than with what is flashing past you. This is the secret of avoiding feeling nauseous or giddy, but if you do feel at all odd return to the crossed arm position and bend your head over until you recover.

Step 4
Your body will automatically take you to the floor when you whirl so fast that you can no longer remain upright. If you are relaxed your body will fall softly. Should this feel threatening, simply slow yourself down gradually, then come to the floor. Lie on your stomach so that you feel completely held by the earth, like an infant cradled by its mother. Remain in this position for 15 minutes. Come back very gradually, making sure that you can be quiet for a while after the meditation.

COMBINING INNER STILLNESS WITH OUTER ACTIVITY

> *How wonderful, how marvellous!*
> *I fetch wood, I carry water.*
>
> P'ang

You may by now be getting the idea that while there are certain techniques that can help us to experience and deepen meditation, *anything* can become a meditation. This is because meditation is about stilling the mind, and coming more and more into the present moment. You are 'coming home' to your innermost core, which doesn't go away simply because you are doing the washing up.

Start by making a physical activity an opportunity for meditating.

Walking

Just walking along, perhaps on the way to work or to the shops, bring your attention to what you are doing. Feel your feet on the ground, the movement of your body, the sights and sounds around you. In particular, notice that you *are* noticing. This is the element of witnessing. Ask yourself 'Who is walking, who is witnessing?'

The Buddhists suggest reminding yourself of what you are doing in a very literal way. Say to yourself, 'Walking, walking, walking' to focus your awareness. The same idea can of course be applied to other activities.

Swimming and floating

Being in water presents a wonderful opportunity for meditation. It is not our usual environment, but there is a certain familiarity. As with the walking meditation, bring your awareness to swimming as though you have never done it before. What's it like before you jump or dive in, then when you enter the water? Feel it against the skin, notice your breathing, any fears or delights, watch the light on the water, listen to the sounds around you.

Try floating. Can you give yourself up to the experience? Keep your attention with what is happening, here and now.

BRINGING MEDITATION INTO EVERYDAY LIFE

Try making some of your absolutely everyday activities into meditations. Be a witness to yourself while you do things for which you normally go on to automatic pilot. Zen Buddhism says, 'Walk or sit – but don't wobble.' In other words, do whatever you are doing totally.

Washing-up

When you've been meditating all day, washing-up becomes a pleasure, a thing in itself not something to be got through.

Dr Susan Blackmore

Washing-up can also become part of your meditation. If, as Dr Blackmore did, you find yourself carrying out such an everyday task at the end of a period of meditation, bring that centredness into the activity. Feel the warm water on your hands, notice the colours in the bubbles and the physical sensations in your body. It becomes a meditation simply by bringing your awareness to it, noticing when other thoughts come in and then returning to the simple task of washing-up.

Driving

Have you ever had the experience of reaching the end of a journey and realising you can't remember driving the last few miles? This happens particularly on regular journeys, such as the one to work. The route is so familiar that there is a tendency to switch off, become immersed in a chain of thoughts and barely notice what you are actually involved in.

When you are driving your main concern is of course safety, but using driving as a meditation will if anything make you an even better driver, more aware of any hazards. The benefits of using it as a meditation are that it reminds you that your inner awareness is precious at any time of day, and in whatever you are doing.

When you are driving:

● Consciously settle yourself into the driving seat before you start the engine, focusing your attention on your breath and what you are about to do.

● While you are driving, whenever possible bring your attention to the act of driving and to what is going on around you.

● Notice when you have driven a few miles and barely seen what you have been driving past.

● Become aware of tensions in your body or your breathing, breathe into them when possible.

● Feel the sensation of the speed of the car.

● Keep coming back to what you are doing, here and now.

● When you reach your destination, check your breathing, relax any tensions, re-connect with the ground as you get out – and move into the next activity.

Smoking

By bringing awareness to something done in a habitual way, great changes become possible. Anyone who smokes will know how hard it is to give up, because apart from the physical effects it becomes firmly ingrained in day-to-day routine.

Instead of trying to just stop smoking – go into it more deeply. Next time you feel like lighting up, notice whether you are just automatically reaching for the packet without making it a conscious act. Then:

● Check whether you really do want a cigarette now, or if it's simply a time or situation when you would usually have one.

- Open the box up with deliberation, making it almost a ritual – feel the paper, smell the cigarette, notice how it feels on your lips, watch the flame as you light it and see the smoke.

- Feel the smoke filling your lungs and being exhaled; are there any emotions, ideas or even memories connected with this? Acknowledge the pleasure you are receiving, as well as any other feelings.

- Make smoking each cigarette a conscious act, so that the habitual aspect of it decreases.

By doing this you are taking charge of what you are doing and feeling. Smoking – or stopping smoking – becomes connected with your intention to create a more calm and centred approach to your life.

Eating
The first step in growth is to do what we love to do and to become aware of doing it.

Sujata

For most people eating is a pleasure as well as a necessity. It can have another dimension too – it is yet another way of using everyday events to bring a sense of reverence and attunement into ordinary acts. The Japanese have done this with their tea ceremony, in which a very normal act is transformed into one of meditation.

Meditating on eating can be not only a lovely experience, but revealing too:

- look at the food before you start eating – become aware of seeing

- reaching out for the food, become aware of your anticipation

- holding the food or the cutlery, become aware of touch

- raising the food to your mouth, become aware of smells and of your body's movement

- putting the food into your mouth, become aware of taste

- chewing the food, become aware of changing tastes and of the mouth's movement

- become aware of swallowing

- become aware of how your desire for another mouthful overtakes you

- become aware of where else your thoughts go, maybe anticipating the next course

- become aware of feelings of greed, or pleasure, or receiving nourishment.

This simple act can highlight feelings, such as fears about not receiving enough, and above all can enhance a part of life often taken for granted. It can make a mundane act one of celebration.

EXPLORING CREATIVITY THROUGH MEDITATION

Parts of the brain (alpha waves) are accessed during meditation which are not normally so readily available. There appears to be a connection between this brain activity and what happens in creative processes. It seems that meditation can increase our creativity – and vice versa.

Painting meditations

Use any art materials that you have to hand: paints, pastels, crayons, felt tips, pens or pencils. Clay can also be used instead. Start each of these sessions by doing a sitting and breathing meditation first, such as the basic meditation.

Art from within

Set up your paper, paints, pencils or whatever you are using before you start meditating. Make the setting up part of your meditation, arranging them with care. Do a sitting meditation as normal. At the end of that time, stay within your meditative state of awareness as much as possible, pick up your paints or pencils, look at the paper, and only make a mark on the paper when you feel ready. It can be any shape. Close your eyes and take a few breaths, open them and look at the first mark you have made, and make another. Make no judgements of what you are doing. Repeat the process until your image feels complete.

Art in the dark

This is a lovely way of letting go of inhibitions about painting or drawing. Set yourself up for the darkness meditation (see page 57) where all light is excluded, and with art materials arranged within reach, and meditate on the breath for a while. Without putting on any light, feel for your paints or pencils, and draw or paint on your paper. Notice if you feel any compulsion to make a 'good' piece of art, and allow yourself to enjoy the act of creativity in this unknown way. You may wish to make several pictures in quick succession. A blindfold can be used instead of a light-fast room if necessary.

QUESTIONS AND ANSWERS

I'd like to try the whirling meditation but I'm scared of falling over or crashing into something.
When you start whirling let your vision whirl too! Don't try to look at any object but see the world spinning around you with a softened focus. That way you will become steady, like the hub of wheel, and will be unlikely to fall. Until you become confident, make sure you have plenty of room around you and some soft cushions on the floor.

Could I use music instead of art as a way of bringing meditation into creativity?
You can follow the same principles as in the art from within meditation, but using an instrument or your voice. Meditate in the usual way for a while, then very slowly make or sing just one note, and slowly let it develop. Whether you are making art or music, this is an excellent way of overcoming inhibitions about feeling 'not artistic' or 'unmusical' as there is no right or wrong outcome, just a delight in creating from your own inner self.

SUMMARY

1. Physical movement can be used as part of a meditation, to energise and release stress. This makes it easier to move into stillness.

2. The movement is part of the meditation too, an opportunity for witnessing and awareness.

3. Everyday activities can become more and more part of a meditative approach to life.

4. Creativity and meditation are close to each other, and one can be used to enhance the other.

8

Relaxing and Meditating

Before me peaceful
Behind me peaceful
Under me peaceful
Over me peaceful
Around me peaceful

(Navajo saying)

Relaxation and meditation: two fine-sounding words which are often thought of as pretty much the same thing. They're not, although there are some overlaps, and some simple relaxation techniques may help you to move into meditation more easily.

COMPARING MEDITATION AND RELAXATION

Relaxation is:

● letting go

● releasing stresses, particularly physical ones

● judging how you feel, then using particular techniques to make changes

whereas meditation is:

● becoming aware

● witnessing what you are thinking, feeling, doing

● non-judgementally waking up to all aspects of yourself without necessarily making changes.

You may well feel more relaxed after meditating, but that's a by-product of becoming more tuned into yourself – tensions and conflicts often melt away by themselves once they are acknowledged. Relaxation is a great way of getting rid of all sorts of stresses and strains, but it will not necessarily bring about a greater inner awareness. Relaxation techniques are very useful though, and can help meditators.

If the difference between meditation and relaxation is still elusive, imagine holding a piece of string by one end. When you let it flop to the ground in loose coils, that's relaxation. When you gently pull it upwards until it hangs straight but loose, that's more like meditation.

RELAXING BEFORE A MEDITATION

If your body is stiff and tense or your breathing tight, it can be difficult to meditate, especially if it's a very still method. There are certain meditations which overcome this by incorporating relaxing sections (see Chapters 6 and 7). Alternatively, you can learn some relaxation techniques to do before you start meditating and at other times of the day. They will ease away physical tension, allowing your inner being some space to come into its own more easily when you begin the meditation.

The **progressive relaxation** below is an excellent basic technique. Other simple methods are outlined later.

PROGRESSIVE RELAXATION

Progressive relaxation is ,an important technique for relaxing the muscles and releasing stress. It also starts giving your mind the message that you intend to relax your thoughts too. Progressive relaxation is based on the idea that by tensing a muscle first, it will relax much more deeply.

Choose a place where you can lie flat, and be warm and comfortable. A bed is not ideal as it is too soft, and you are likely to connect it with going to sleep. Try the floor with a soft blanket or mat on it.

- Lie down on your back and close your eyes. Move yourself around a bit until you feel comfortable, then lie still.

- Inhale and raise your right leg a few inches off the floor, tensing the muscles in it. Hold it for a few seconds, then let it drop back to the floor as you breathe out. It is important to feel the leg sinking into the floor before you start the next section, and this applies with each part of the relaxation.

- Now repeat the leg-tensing and relaxing with the left leg, then your arms and buttocks.

- Breathe in deeply, push your abdomen out like a balloon. Hold this for a few seconds, tensing the abdomen, then release the breath as fully as you can.

- Do the same with the upper chest.

- Shrug your shoulders up to your ears, then bring them forward towards your chest, then push them down towards your feet. And relax.

- Roll your head gently from side to side, releasing tension in the neck.

- Breathe in, and tense up all the muscles in your face. Screw up your eyes, move your jaw around, make as many facial contortions as you can – no one will see! Exhale and let the facial muscles fall away as though your face has been smoothed over. Don't forget the muscles in the scalp and around the ears.

- Get a sense of the whole body, feeling it relaxing more. Notice any parts which still feel tense or stiff, breathe into them and feel them relaxing more. Continue this for a while – make sure you give yourself enough time and don't rush off before you're really ready. This is time for you. Come out of the relaxation by deepening your breathing, stretching slowly, moving and slowly sitting up.

- Notice if you feel different from before you started. This is important as it reinforces your resolution to relax and meditate if you can be aware of changes.

USING RELAXATION TECHNIQUES

Stretching
The first step towards finding greater inner peace is to quieten down the body. Stretching and lengthening the muscles helps counteract chronic stiffness, and restore health to body and mind. **Hatha yoga** has many excellent postures for promoting muscle stretch. You can also just make sure that you stretch your body throughout the day – take some lessons from the cat! If you are desk-bound, the following basic routine is useful.

Head rotations

- Sit comfortably. Inhale, then as you exhale allow your head to gently fall as close to your chest as feels comfortable.

- Feel the stretch in your shoulders and the back of the neck.

- Bring your head back up and relax.

● Without bringing your shoulder up to your ear, lower your right ear towards your right shoulder.

● Very slowly and gently rotate your head backwards and around in a circle, gently exhaling and allowing the face and jaw to relax, finishing where you began.

Do the same with the left ear and shoulder, and repeat several times on each side.

Relaxing the eyes
A lot of tension develops in the eyes, especially with the coming of computers and TV. This simple exercise, like the one above, can be done as part of a pre-meditation process or even when you're sitting at your desk.

Palming
Rub the palms of your hands together vigorously until you have generated some heat in them. Cup them over your eyes, feeling the heat from your palms warming and relaxing your eyes. Keep them there until you feel you need to re-warm your hands, and repeat as often as you like.

As an optional extra, after palming you can ease more tension from the eyes by firmly stroking the eyebrows from the inside towards the outer edge.

Breathing
The breath is the bridge between the body and the mind – one can affect the other. Learning some breathing techniques is an excellent way of using the body to calm the mind, and vice versa. When you are anxious, your breath is shallow and rapid, increasing:

● heart rate

● blood pressure

● muscular tension.

When you are relaxed you breathe more slowly and deeply, producing:

● a calming effect on mind and body

● a decrease in nervous-system stimulation.

Deep breathing
Deep breathing is another technique that can be used in everyday situations as well as during your relaxation session.

- Breathe out through your nose. Now start inhaling by filling your abdomen with air. Let the air rise up through your body – the lower chest expands and you feel the air rising higher, up into the top of the lungs until you feel your collar-bones rising.

- Exhale, breathing out through your nose. Take longer over this than the inhale, because you are letting go of tension. A ratio of 2:1 is good. Feel the breath deepening as you continue the breaths.

Return to normal breathing if you feel dizzy or short of breath.

QUESTIONS AND ANSWERS

Can I combine a relaxation with meditation?
Doing a relaxation before a meditation is a good idea, especially if it's a sitting meditation. But be quite clear about whether you are relaxing or meditating. Relaxing is a dreamy state, whereas meditating is completely awake. After you have relaxed your body with one of the techniques suggested, consciously bring your attention back to a state of alertness, ready for meditation.

SUMMARY

1. Relaxation techniques can be used to release physical stress and tension.

2. Meditation eventually leads to a relaxed state of being, but using some relaxation techniques in addition will make it easier to access this inner stillness.

9

Using Other Techniques
to Help Meditation

The breeze at dawn has secrets to tell you. Don't go back to sleep.
You must ask for what you really want. Don't go back to sleep.
People are going back and forth across the doorsill
where the two worlds touch.
The door is round and open. Don't go back to sleep!

Rumi

As you become more used to meditating you may find a new way of seeing the world – and yourself – opening up. It might start with quite simple things, such as becoming aware, through sitting, of some backache you hadn't given enough attention to before. Or it could be that through meditating you see your thoughts often go to a particular problem area in your life. Perhaps you simply find that meditating has turned a key in a lock and you would like to find out more about other aspects of your self.

There are many methods which you can use in this journey of self-discovery, all of which will enhance your meditation in various ways. They range from physical techniques such as massage, aromatherapy, yoga and t'ai chi, to those dealing with feelings, such as counselling. Their relevance to meditation is that they offer a way of releasing distractions, such as physical aches or emotional pains, and also encourage awareness and inner attention. Some of the most relevant ones are outlined in this chapter.

LOOKING AT GUIDED VISUALISATION

A **guided visualisation** is a journey that you take in your imagination. Its purpose is to provide you with an experience in which you can 're-programme' or discover something about yourself.

Visualisation is sometimes confused with meditation, because it happens within the mind. They are really quite different:

- in meditation you are cultivating a choiceless awareness of whatever happens

- in visualisation you are providing your mind with very specific input.

Humans have developed incredibly sophisticated languages, but the way we *see* the world is probably much more fundamental. Perhaps this is why it has been proved that the *body* responds to images as though they were actually happening. Visualisation – imagining certain images or scenes – can produce measurable changes in the body. For instance, a psychologist recorded the muscle activity of a skier who was just imagining himself racing downhill, and found that these recordings were similar to those taken when he was actually skiing.

Visualisation can help meditators by:

- taking you on a different kind of journey into new aspects of your self

- providing a way of releasing emotional conflicts and accessing peaceful feelings

- confirming your intention to work with your innermost self

- discovering your creativity and imagination, and taking strength from this in your resolution to go deeper into meditation.

TRYING SOME GUIDED VISUALISATIONS

The sample guided visualisation which follows is a way of contacting your inner resources and gaining a new insight into your life. It is also very revealing about yourself and, like most guided visualisations, highly pleasurable. It can help deepen your meditation as it opens up parts of your being which tend to be swamped in everyday existence.

You can read the guided visualisation through before doing it and simply remember it. Ideally, though, record it on audio cassette so that you can really relax into it and get the most from it. Do the visualisation lying down in a warm place with your eyes closed, deepening the breath and relaxing before you begin.

A Journey

It is a fine, fresh morning in early summer. Coming out of your house you feel the gentle warmth of the rising sun on your face. You walk on the grass, the dew wet on your feet and sparkling in the early morning light. The fresh air seems to hold a promise, an invitation for an adventure. As you hear the birds calling each other you decide that this is the perfect day for a journey you have long wanted to undertake.

You set off down the road from your house. Rounding the corner, the sea comes into sight. It looks lovelier than you have ever seen it – a deep blue, promising a day of sunshine. Already some boats are bobbing far out at sea and seagulls are circling overhead. You smell the salt in the air and feel the breeze fresher on your face.

On the horizon you see the tiny dot of an island in the sea. You have seen this island for so long, and longed to go there. Today is the day you have decided to make the journey and you gaze with anticipation at the shimmering, distant speck of land.

As you approach the harbour from which you will sail, you see that some of the people you love best in the world are gathered there, right on the quay. They seem to have known about your special journey, and have come to give you a wonderful send-off.

A small boat pulls into the quayside: the boat which is going to take you to the island. You say goodbye to your friends or family, noting how you feel about leaving them behind – for somehow you know that this is a journey which you must undertake alone – and get into the boat. You look at the boatman who is going to take you across the water – do you already know him, is he familiar, or quite unknown and even mysterious?

The journey across the water is exciting. Diamonds of light flash off the crests of the waves as the boat ploughs through and picks up speed. The sounds and smells of the sea are all around you. You lie back on brightly coloured, soft silk cushions as the boatman guides the vessel across the sea. The land you have come from grows distant and faint, until you can no longer see the people who came to wave you goodbye. You draw nearer and nearer to the island you have looked at so longingly for such a long time. The land is becoming clearer, and you see that it is fringed by white beaches and woodland above which a mountain peak rises, so high that it is capped with snow.

As you approach the island brightly coloured birds fly out to greet you, squawking, and rainbow-coloured fish leap in arcs from the water as though to celebrate your long-awaited arrival.

At last you are here. The boat floats into shallow azure waters bounded by a white sand beach and dense trees. The boatman helps you ashore and you thank him for getting you here safely, knowing he will be waiting for you and your safe return. The next part of the journey will be by yourself.

You look around, noticing the thick woodland. Some of the trees are types completely unknown to you, some are familiar. There is a feeling of abundance and vitality, and the smells now are woody and earthy. You hear animals calling and birds singing, and though you feel some trepidation you long to explore. Ahead of you a narrow path leads through the jungly woodland. Following it, you find that the ground rises steadily, steeper and steeper. It is becoming hot and steamy in this luminous green forest.

As you begin to wonder where you are heading, the thick woodland suddenly opens up and you find yourself on a rocky path. Above you the mountain soars upwards – suddenly so much closer – and beneath you the wood through which you have just toiled is spread out like a velvety green cushion. You can even make out the boat moored by the beach, still just close enough to see the boatman giving you a reassuring wave. The wave is welcome, as you gaze up at the mountain and know that you have no choice but to climb to the top of it.

Your path now winds up and up, around the side of the mountain. The lush green woodland is left behind, and the path becomes narrow and rocky. But even here small plants grow and jewel-like flowers delight you with their tiny blossoms. The temperature is dropping; you wrap yourself in a warm sweater. Now you are so high above the hazy clouds that you can no longer see the boat, the sea or even the woods. You feel completely alone.

As you turn the next corner of the path you see a lake set into the mountainside. It is absolutely still, its glassy surface reflecting the crystal clarity of the sky. Standing on the side of the lake you look at yourself reflected in its surface. You see yourself with greater clarity than ever before. As you gaze at yourself you feel a great love and compassion for this person you see, for the face with all the feelings it expresses and for the body which has brought you all this way. The stillness and clarity of the water in which you see your reflection seem to wash over and through you.

You dip your hand into the water. The waters break and your reflection disappears. Drinking the pure water from your cupped hand you give thanks for the liquid which seems to fill every part of your body with a renewed energy.

The mountain top is growing nearer. Your path now takes you along the side of a rushing mountain river which courses over rocks and waterfalls. The sound of the water, and its spray which mists your face, help you find the energy to climb the last bit of the mountain. By now you are in the snow, and your feet crunch into the fresh covering on the path.

You are there at last, the top of the mountain. You find a rock to sit on which feels almost as comfortable as an armchair. Resting into it you get your breath back and feel a sense of achievement. Now you can look around you – back at the path you have just climbed, then at what lies beneath you, laid out like a carpet at your feet. The clouds have cleared and you can make out the rest of the island and the sea. In the far distance you can just make out the land from which you sailed this morning. Take your time to take in every detail of the landscape and congratulate yourself on your achievement. Feel the purity of the air on your skin, listen to the distant sounds of the rushing water and the call of birds. You are completely alone in this distant place yet your connections with the rest of the world are still there. You are absolutely at ease.

Spend as long here as you need to. When the time is right your journey back begins. But as you climb down from the rock to rejoin the path you notice a large crack in the rock-face, and decide to look inside. The narrow, dark opening widens into a large cavern, the walls covered in a myriad of shiny rocks and crystals which flash with brilliant colours. You feel as though you are being bathed in light and colour. Then in the corner of the cavern you see a small wooden box. To your surprise it has your name on it, and you know there is a very special gift in here for you. Opening the box you see ... what? Perhaps a small, precious object which has a meaning for you, maybe something more abstract like a feeling or an idea. Whatever it is, it is yours to take home with you. You give thanks for it.

The journey back down the mountainside is easy. The rushing stream accompanies you, your step is light. You pass the still lake again, and notice any differences in your appearance – perhaps it is your expression, or a new lightness in your body. Down through the woodland, and the shore comes into sight. There is your boat, with the boatman waiting to take you back on board and sail back home.

As you settle back into the silk cushions you feel completely calm and peaceful. You have a sense of achievement, of having climbed this high mountain by yourself, of seeing sights and hearing sounds you never knew before. You recall the vision you had of yourself in the clear lake, and the treasure you have brought with you from the cavern. As you approach the land you see your loved ones gathered there to meet you again. Before you step ashore you thank the boatman for his care, and you take one last look back at the island, thanking yourself for the courage and trust you had in yourself to make this journey. You hold the treasure you have brought back with you, and step ashore.

Understanding a guided visualisation

The visualisation above could be said to help you access some of the higher aspects of your self, especially as it involves a journey away from your normal life. The lake might represent a clear, seeing part of yourself, the mountain top your spiritual, higher being and so on. However, there is no need to intellectually understand the meaning of guided visualisations, especially as they are often about getting in touch with parts of ourselves which are more to do with feelings and spirit than with the mind. The only true way of judging them is whether they leave you feeling refreshed or helped in some way.

RELEASING ANXIETY THROUGH VISUALISATION

Clear water visualisation

This purifying visualisation can be used to drain away stress and anxiety, leaving you feeling freer of anything that is constricting you.

Step 1
Sit quietly with your eyes closed. Starting from the top of the head imagine clear, cool water filling your body. See it slowly moving into every space within the body – down through the chest to the pelvis, from shoulders to fingertips, from pelvis to toes.

Step 2
Now that you are 'filled' with this crystal-clear water, imagine the room you are sitting in filling with water too, slowly rising from the floor up to the ceiling.

Step 3
Let the water you are visualising in the room drain away, from the ceiling to the floor, until none is left.

Step 4
Imagine the purifying water leaving the body, draining from the feet up into the torso, arms and head. As you see the last drop leaving the top of the skull, feel the anxieties and stresses that were troubling you leaving with the water. See the water evaporate and disappear into the atmosphere, taking your concerns with it.

DEVELOPING YOUR OWN VISUALISATIONS

Guided visualisations are as limitless as your own imagination. You can devise your own ones according to your particular needs, following the principles outlined above. You can also use visualisation to help address particular issues. For instance, to assist with creativity you can visualise a bridge connecting the left and right sides of your brain; to feel refreshed and cleansed you could take yourself on a windy, sunlit journey involving waterfalls and rivers; for relaxation you might visualise being wrapped in a warm pink cloud; an imaginary journey to a beach could have you stripping off for a swim to help build a more positive body image, and so on.

Using visualisation in everyday life

Most visualisations are done lying down with closed eyes, but there is a very useful technique which can be used at any time. Identify a mental picture which is relevant to you at the moment for some reason; it might for example be a mountain-top, or a stream, a dancing figure, a heart, a healthy body, a ray of sunlight, or someone sitting in meditation. Whatever it is, simply bring this into your thoughts like a snapshot several times a day. It doesn't need to interfere with whatever you are doing, you see it for a split second and release it, knowing it is affirming whatever that image represents for you.

USING OTHER SELF-HELP METHODS

Today a dazzling array of complementary therapies and ancient techniques for growth and health is available. The ones listed below are some most likely to be helpful for meditation.

Aromatherapy

Essential oils extracted from plants have been used for thousands of years to promote health and well-being. Aromatherapy has become one of the most widely used complementary therapies, probably because it is not only very accessible but also enjoyable. Oils can be applied through massage, in a bath or inhaled in a vaporiser. Certain oils are particularly helpful for meditation:

- olibanum (or frankincense), said to deepen meditation
- sandalwood, also traditionally used for meditation
- lavender to aid relaxation
- lemongrass for alertness.

Alexander technique

A very gentle system of body alignment and release. The practitioner (teacher) gently guides the student to lengthen and balance the body, and encouragement is given to maintain this bodily poise and ease in everyday life. Almost a meditation in itself.

Art therapy

A creative way of accessing and expressing feelings. Working individually or in groups, the art therapist offers support in overcoming obstacles to self-expression, allowing ideas and emotions to be resolved in a way which may be beyond words. A way of working with the inner self.

Autogenics
A systematised approach to relaxation, geared towards people with busy lives. Once you have learnt the system you spend just seven minutes, three times a day practising it. The principle behind autogenics is that the mind can be used to relax the body. It is taught as an eight-week course, covering physical calming, slowing the heart beat and easing the solar plexus which is seen as the seat of tension.

Counselling/psychotherapy
If you find that difficult emotional issues are coming to the fore in your meditation, and do not seem to be resolving themselves, it could be helpful to have some counselling or psychotherapy. Sessions should help you understand the disturbance, leading to a clearer space for meditation.

Flotation
Floating in a completely dark, body-temperature pool is quite an experience. A soundproof flotation pool is filled with body-supporting salts, so that you have a sensation of being weightless. It is deeply relaxing, and can also be used as a great place to do the darkness meditation.

Massage
Stimulates and relaxes muscles, detoxifies the body and restores a sense of physical harmony. By receiving a massage you also become aware of your body, as you lie with closed eyes. An excellent aid to meditation.

Self-hypnosis
Hypnotherapy has become well known, especially for helping with giving up smoking, losing weight, treating phobias etc. Self-hypnosis goes even deeper, and you can 'programme' yourself safely to go very deeply into meditation. The techniques involved are relaxing and enjoyable; you will need to find a local teacher or practitioner.

Shamanism
Based on tribal meditations, often from the American Indian tradition. Drumming and chanting may be used to induce a meditative trance. It is

particularly concerned with deepening our understanding of our place within nature. The connection with meditation is in taking responsibility for your life by going deeply inside yourself. A path to be followed over a long period of time, but you can get a taste at workshops.

T'ai Chi

Traditional Chinese movement meditation. The gentle movements are not only extremely beneficial to agility and health generally, but encourage a state of awareness and meditation. You need to be taught t'ai chi, but can then practise it on your own.

Yoga

Yoga is another ancient way of bringing awareness to the self through the body. There are many types of yoga; in the West we are most familiar with hatha yoga which deals primarily with postures and breathing. There are many other forms, some focusing much more on the spirit and meditation.

QUESTIONS AND ANSWERS

How do I find a practitioner or teacher for any of these methods?
Contact your local complementary health centre, see Useful Addresses or, best of all, get a personal recommendation for a practitioner or teacher. Books and tapes will help you learn some of them, but personal experience is the best. Your local NHS health centre may also have names of counsellors, psychotherapists, art therapists and masseurs.

SUMMARY

1. Using other techniques can help overcome difficulties which arise in meditation.

2. Meditating can open up a whole new world of physical, mental, spiritual and emotional discovery which can be further explored through treatments, techniques and therapies. They in turn help deepen meditation further.

10

Meditating with Others

When you practise these precious teachings, slowly the clouds of sorrow melt away. And the sun of wisdom and true joy will be shining in the clear sky of your mind.

Kalu Rinpoche

There are many different ways of learning to meditate. You can use a book – an excellent way to get going at your own pace – or follow a meditation tape or CD. Most people at some time or other will benefit from working with an experienced teacher of meditation. The benefits of doing this are:

- Although meditation is essentially very simple and straightforward, it can be inspiring and encouraging to work with someone who has been there already, knows the pitfalls, and will find ways of helping you through particular difficulties.

You will most probably be meditating with other people. This can be not only encouraging, but often very powerful as the meditative energy of a whole group of people develops.

JOINING A MEDITATION GROUP

Meditation groups range from the formal to the group-of-friends-getting-together category. There are also many introductory sessions around the country, where you can drop in without obligation to see if it is what you want.

Established meditation courses

- Many local education authorities run courses in meditation. Ask at your local library, college or bookshop for help with finding a teacher or group.

- There are several Buddhist Centres in London (see Useful Addresses), running drop-in evening and daytime courses, as well as ongoing courses, weekend and day retreats. They give a complete grounding in meditation, including posture, preparation, techniques and dealing with distractions.

● Transcendental Meditation Courses are run at 60 centres around the country. At the time of going to press they cost £490, or £290 concessionary rate.

● See Useful Addresses for contacts for other meditation organisations.

Setting up your own group

Meditating with others is very supportive. You are making a regular commitment and sharing the experience. If you have one or more friends or acquaintances who are also interested in meditation, suggest meeting once a week. It can be an excellent chance to try out new meditations, perhaps taking it in turns to decide which meditation to do. Allow time at the end to talk about your experiences, and make it an enjoyable, social event.

MEDITATING AS A GROUP

Most meditations, even when done alongside other people, are essentially solitary experiences. Just a few are done as part of a group process where the participants interact with each other.

Circle dancing

This is a type of movement meditation, but one that you can only do with other people. Participants form a circle, and are taught the steps. Once the music starts the routine is repeated again and again, until the steps become absolutely automatic. Initially you have to concentrate hard on getting the movements right, thus helping the mind's usual chattering to quieten down. But then comes a release and the body flows with the movement, the music and the other dancers.

One circle dancer comments, 'There's something about some of the movements that evokes a really deep peace in a way that being still with your own thoughts doesn't achieve, the music is filling you with peace rather than leaving you trying to find it.'

Dances for Universal Peace (see Useful Addresses) will also give an experience of circle dance meditation.

MEDITATING WITH A FRIEND OR PARTNER

Meditating with someone you are close to can bring you together in quiet harmony, and will add depth to your meditation experience.

Nadabrahma for couples
This is a variation on the Tibetan humming meditation (page 69).

Step 1
Light four candles in the meditation room, and also light some incense or burn essential oil that you use only for this meditation.

Step 2
Sit facing your partner, as close as possible and holding each other's crossed hands. Drape a light sheet right over you both, to concentrate your energies. Follow the first (humming) part of the meditation, feeling yourselves gradually merging.

Step 3
Stay sitting together for a while longer, until the time feels right to finish. Thank your partner.

Gazing
This is simply a variation on the other gazing meditations – but gazing at your friend or partner is quite different from gazing at a candle!

Step 1
Sit close to each other, facing but not touching. Keep your eyes open and take a few slow, deep breaths.

Step 2
Gaze at each other's left eye. Let your gaze be gentle, try not to blink much. Notice any thoughts or feelings that arise, and feel yourself melting into the gaze. Your breathing may naturally fall into harmony with each other. Maintain this for at least ten minutes.

Step 3
Close your eyes, sit together quietly for a few minutes before finishing.

MEDITATING WITH CHILDREN

Many children have a lot to cope with these days, and meditation can be a valuable tool in their self-development, providing moral and spiritual support and a way to deal with emotions. For parents and teachers it can also be a way of connecting with children in a different way from usual. Many parents feel it provides their children with a valuable, lifetime inner resource.

Some people might feel that meditating with children is imposing something on them, but meditation is not a cult and does not have to be tied to any particular religion or philosophy. Children can be free to choose whether they wish to pursue it or not.

Any of the meditations in this book can be used, depending on the age of the children. Start simply, such as with the Basic Meditation. However, do make the meditations short – maybe just a few minutes to begin with. Allow the children time to talk about their experiences, and suggest making it a regular part of their everyday routine.

Teaching meditation to lively children

Meditation may be particularly useful for children showing signs of attention deficit disorder. Journalist Deanne Pearson wrote of her own experience: 'My seven-year-old son has always been lively and had a short attention span which his classmates sometimes found disruptive. However, since I started teaching him to meditate a few months ago he has really settled down and is able to concentrate for much longer periods.'

In *Teaching Meditation to Children*, author David Fontana comments that while parents might worry that their particularly active children may not be able to stay still for long enough, it is often these children who take to it most easily.

GOING ON A MEDITATION RETREAT

Retreats are an extended period of time out of your normal, everyday existence. They have long been practised by most religions, but they do not need to have a religious connotation. It is now possible to find many retreats aimed at secular as well as religious meditators. Some of them will teach a particular form of meditation. Going on a meditation retreat can be an excellent way of:

● starting meditation, learning the basics with experienced practitioners

● or deepening your existing practice by learning new methods, sharing experiences with other meditators and simply having an extended period of time meditating.

A retreat could be as short as a day or two, maybe a week or even months! One meditator who took part in a twelve-day retreat commented, 'It was one of the best experiences in my life. It wasn't always at all easy, it took a lot of determination. But I learnt such a lot about myself, I found a new strength and insight, a greater connection with life. It gave me a taste of what meditation is about that I don't think I would have had by just meditating briefly every day. Even though it was some time ago, I can still feel its effects because it gave me such a new experience. It may sound corny but it changed my life!'

Buddhist retreats

A Buddhist retreat could be a good way of learning or practising meditation, even if you are not a Buddhist. The Friends of the Western Buddhist Order (see Useful Addresses) run occasional retreats and stress that the focus is on meditation rather than Buddhism. They say, 'A Buddhist retreat is an ideal situation in which to take a fresh look at yourself and your life. On retreat you can relax and enjoy yourself. You can learn to meditate, or take your meditation further with the help of experienced teachers. This can help you develop clarity, confidence, emotional positivity and even a deeper insight into yourself. A retreat is an ideal situation in which you can grow.'

The Samye-Ling Tibetan Centre in Scotland also runs introductory courses.

Other retreats

A wide range of current meditation retreats can be found listed in magazines such as those in Further Reading. Your local church should be able to provide information about Christian-based retreats.

GOING ABROAD

There are two main reasons, broadly speaking, why you might choose to travel to another country as part of your meditation development.

1. To go to a country where the particular type of meditation you are interested in is widely practised.

2. To include meditation as part of your holiday.

In the first case you might, for instance, travel to Japan to practise Zen Buddhism, to India for Hindu meditation in an ashram, and so on. For the second option you might prefer to spend just a part of your holiday meditating, and may never have done any before. There are now many specialist companies running tours to sacred sites, and there are plenty of holiday centres abroad specialising in holidays which combine inner growth with just having a great time. For up-to-date information consult one of the periodicals listed in Further Reading, or contact the following from Useful Addresses:

– Osho Commune, India – meditation in an ashram
– Skyros holidays including meditation in Greece and the Caribbean
– Sivananda Yoga Vedanta Centre – yoga/meditation camps abroad
– Cortijo Romero – holidays including meditation in Spain.

MEDITATING IN A RELIGIOUS CONTEXT

This book has emphasised the fact that meditation does not need to be linked to any religion or spiritual movement. However, you might wish to meditate with others by linking it with your own religious following. In the UK today Christianity offers a meditative tradition, and Buddhism is becoming increasingly popular as a spiritual path (though it does claim not to be a religion!).

Christianity

Christianity has contemplative practices which are certainly meditations. Some of these are similar to mantras. For example:

● The 5th-century Diadochus of Photice and 7th-century John Climacus recommended repeating the name of Jesus.

● The Jesus Prayer has been used by Orthodox monks for centuries as a way of concentrating the attention (see mantras, page 54). It was used in the system of Christian mysticism developed by the monks of Mount Athos in the 14th century.

● An unknown 14th-century monk wrote in *The Cloud of Unknowing*: 'Take a short word, preferably of one syllable … the shorter the word the better, being more like the meaning of the Spirit; a word like "God" or "love". Choose one which you like, or perhaps some other so long as it is of one syllable. And fix this word fast to your heart, so that it is always there come what may. It will be your shield and spear in peace and war alike. With this word you will suppress all thought under the cloud of forgetting.'

Meditation in Christianity today
The contemplative dimension of Christianity has been acknowledged in recent years through the work of various teachers who have taught meditation. One such teacher was John Main who is said to have opened up the monastic tradition of 'pure prayer' – or meditation – to people living in the world. His emphasis has been on meditation as a spiritual discipline, not merely a technique. Main's work has provided the inspiration for The World Community for Christian Meditation, a 'monastery without walls' with members around the world (see Useful Addresses).

The Quakers' prayer meetings, where silent contemplation is practised, is also within the meditative tradition.

Buddhism
Buddhism has become increasingly popular in the West in the last few years. The list of actors and actresses, pop stars and celebrities who are said to practice Buddhism seems to grow every day. Perhaps because Buddhism does not demand a belief in God, its tenets can be used as a way of living.

The Friends of the Western Buddhist Order, for instance, say, 'Buddhism provides people with a straightforward approach to change. Blind belief plays no part at all. The only faith one needs is in one's own ability to develop. All Buddhist teachings and practices are means to enable us to grow into states of ever increasing happiness and creativity, to fulfil our highest potential and reach what Buddhism calls Enlightenment.'

The Friends of the Western Buddhist Order
Founded in 1967 by Sangharakshita, an English Buddhist monk who had spent 20 years in India practising, studying and teaching Buddhism. When he came back to the West he felt that things could improve in the Buddhist scene, and founded the FWBO to transmit the essentials of Buddhism in a way relevant to the modern West. This is now the largest Buddhist group in the UK, with centres throughout the world (see Useful Addresses).

QUESTIONS AND ANSWERS
Can you suggest a final meditation?
Laugh. Meditation is not such a serious matter. If it has any 'purpose' it must be to connect us with bliss and joy. So as soon as you awake in the morning start laughing, just for the sheer delight of being alive.

SUMMARY

Meditating with other people is a good way of moving on in meditation, providing new ideas, insights and encouragement. Consider finding or even starting a local group so that meditation remains a fresh and wonderful voyage of discovery.

Glossary

Affirmation. A positive statement designed to produce a desired outcome, usually repeated many times.

Alpha waves. Brain waves associated with relaxed, creative states and which are now known to be encouraged through meditation.

Attention. Central to meditation. By focusing the mind's attention on something such as the breath or a candle flame the meditator becomes more aware.

Breath. Focusing on the breath is used in many meditation techniques as a way of stilling the mind and providing a focal point for the attention.

Chakras. Seven energy centres located throughout the body and associated with specific organs, functions, colours, emotions.

Concentration. Often confused with meditation, but more sharp and precise, usually to do with working on a particular task. Meditation aims for a softer, more generalised awareness.

Conscious dreaming. Having some awareness of and control over dreams as they happen.

Dhikr. Similar to a mantra, practised in Sufism.

Fight-or-flight response. The body's natural response to any stressful experience. We may have lost the art of recovering from this response, to the detriment of our health. The stress this produces can be dealt with through meditation. (See also **relaxation response**.)

Guided visualisation. An imaginary journey, scene or image in which positive thoughts may be encouraged and discoveries made about the self.

Focus. The object, act or sensation used in a meditation as the point to which the attention is returned, e.g. the breath, a flame, walking, even washing-up.

Incense. The herbs and spices used to make incense sticks or cones give off pungent smells when burnt, which are said to aid meditation.

Kundalini. A spiritual energy or life-force, also known as serpent power, which is said to reside in the spinal column and can be activated through meditation.

Latihan. A letting go into the energy of the body and spirit.

Loving kindness meditation (or **metta bhavana**). An ancient Buddhist meditation centred on the heart.

Mandala. An image used for meditating on, having a central focus from which patterns or pictures radiate.

Mantra. A single, repeated word or phrase used to focus the attention.

Meditation space. A place arranged for meditation, according to taste and needs. Using one particular place regularly helps enter into meditation more easily.

Metta bhavana meditation. See **loving kindness**.

Mindfulness meditation. A form of vipassana or awareness meditation, but focused on whatever sensations are happening rather than just on the breath.

Mudra. A particular meditation position denoting surrender.

Nadabrahma meditation. An ancient Tibetan humming meditation.

Naming. A method used particularly in breath meditations, where a train of thought is 'named' so that it can be noted and then moved on from.

Relaxation response. The opposite of the fight-or-flight response. Identified by Benson as the body's natural way of recuperating, but disallowed in recent times thus building up physical, mental and emotional stress.

Sacred space. See **meditation space**.

Transcendental meditation (TM). A form of meditation using **mantras**, made popular in the West by the Beatles.

Tratak. Gazing meditations.

Vipassana. An age-old Buddhist meditation, now also widely practised in the West. The essence of vipassana is awareness, and it often uses the breath as a focal point.

Visualisation. See **guided visualisation**.

Witnessing. Becoming aware of what you are doing in a non-judgmental, passive way.

Zazen. A Buddhist form of meditation in which the eyes are kept open. The gaze is soft and diffused, not concentrated on any particular object.

Zen. A Japanese form of Buddhism in which meditation plays an important part. It describes meditation as 'Sitting quietly, doing nothing'.

Useful Addresses

Amitabha Buddhist Centre, St Audries House, West Quantoxhead, Taunton TA4 4DU. Tel: (01984) 633200.
  E-mail: amitabha@rmplc.co.uk. Residential Buddhist college and retreat centre, beginners and experienced.
The Barn, Lower Sharpham Barton, Ashprington, Totnes, Devon TQ9 7DX. Tel: (01803) 732661. Fax: (01803) 732037. Meditation practice; exploring community living.
Barry Long Foundation. Tel: (01442) 877530. Meditation courses.
Brahma Kumaris, Global Co-operation House, 65 Pound Lane, London NW1O 2HH. Tel: (0181) 459 1400. Meditation courses.
Bristol Buddhist Centre, 162 Gloucester Road, Bishopston, Bristol. Tel: (0117) 924 9991.
British Association for Autogenic Training and Therapy, 18 Holtsmere Close, Watford, Herts WD2 6NG. Send SAE for list of trainers.
British Association for Counselling, 1 Regent Place, Rugby, Warwickshire CV21 2PJ. Tel (01788) 550899. Send SAE for practitioners list.
British Association of Art Therapists, Mary Ward House, 5 Tavistock Place, London WC1H 9SN. Tel: (0171) 383 3774. Information and list of members.
British Hypnotherapy Association, 67 Upper Berkeley Street, London W1H 7DH. Tel: (0171) 723 4443.
The British Wheel of Yoga, 1 Hamilton Place, Boston Road, Sleaford, Lincolnshire NG34 7ES. Tel: (01529) 306851.
Centre for Complementary Health Studies, Exeter University Foundation, Freepost, Exeter EX1 1AZ. Degree courses.
Centre for Health & Healing, St James's Church, 197 Piccadilly, London W1. Long established centre, includes some meditation sessions.
Chetan Woodwork, The Roundhouse, Buckland in the Moor, Ashburton, Devon TQ13 7HN. Maker and supplier of meditation stools.
Complementary Medicine Association (CMA), 142 Greenwich High Road, London SE10 8NN. Tel: (0181) 305 9571. Can refer you to a registered practitioner.

Cortijo Romero, Little Grove, Grove Lane, Chesham, Bucks HP5 3QQ. Tel: (01494) 78270. Fax: (01494) 776066. Alternative holidays in Spain.

Dances of Universal Peace, Penny Farm Cottage, Holwell, Sherborne, Dorset DT9 5LJ. Tel: (01963) 23124. Meditative circle dancing.

Dharmachakra, PO Box 50, Cambridge CB1 3BG. Tapes on Buddhism and meditation. Free catalogue.

Eagle's Wing Centre for Contemporary Shamanism. Tel: (0171) 435 8174.

The Float Information Service. Tel: (0171) 357 0302.

Friends of the Western Buddhist Order. See London Buddhist Centre; for your nearest centre contact them or see your local phone book.

Gaunts House, Wimborne, Dorset BH21 4JQ. Tel: (01202) 841522. Workshops and retreats.

Grimstone Manor, Yelverton, Devon PL2O 7QY. Tel: (01822) 854358. Residential workshops.

Gurdjieff Ouspensky Centres. London: (0181) 347 5353. Edinburgh: (0141) 889 8044. Meditation classes.

Hawkwood College, Painswick Old Road, Stroud, Glos GL6 7QW. Tel: (01453) 759034. Fax: (01453) 764607. Courses including meditation.

Hazelwood House, Loddiswell, Nr Kingsbridge, South Devon TQ7 4EB. Tel: (01548) 821232. Fax: (01548) 821318. Programme of residential workshops.

London Buddhist Centre, 51 Roman Road, London E2 OHU. Tel: (0181) 981 1225. Regular introductions to meditation. Part of the Friends of the Western Buddhist Order.

The Massage Training Institute, 24 Highbury Grove, London N5 2DQ. National register.

Monkton Wyld Court, Bridport, Dorset DT6 6DQ. Tel: (01297) 560342. Fax: (01297) 560395. E-mail: monktonwyldcourt@btinternet.com. Retreats and various therapies.

National Council of Psychotherapists, Head Office, Hazelwood, Broadmead, Sway, Lymington, Hants S041 6DH. Tel: (01590) 683770. Send SAE for list.

National Federation of Spiritual Healers, Old Manor Farm Studio, Church St, Sunbury-on-Thames, Middlesex TWI6 6RG. Tel: (01932) 783164.

North London Buddhist Centre, St Marks Studio, London N7 8SJ. Tel: (0171) 700 3075.

Osho Commune International, 17 Koregoan Park, Poona 411 001, India. Meditation ashram, including introductory courses.

Osho Purnima Distribution, Greenwise, Vange Park Road, Basildon, Essex SS16 5LA. Tel: (01268) 584141.
E-mail: OshoPurnima@compuserve.com. Books and tapes.

Portman Lodge, Durweston, Blandford, Dorset DT11 0QA.
Tel: (01258) 452168. Fax: (01258) 450456. Courses including meditation.

Positive Health Centre for Autogenic Training. Tel: (0171) 935 1811.

The Professional Association of Alexander Teachers. Tel: (0121) 4262108. Practitioners throughout UK.

Register of Qualified Aromatherapists, PO Box 3431, Danbury, Chelmsford, Essex CM3 4UA. Tel: (01245) 227957. List of local practitioners.

The Sacred Trust, PO Box 603, Bath, Somerset BA1 2ZU. Tel: (01225) 852615. Shamanic practitioners.

Samye-Ling Tibetan Centre, Eskdalemuir, Scotland DG13 0QL.
Tel: (013873) 73232. Residential meditation courses and retreats.

Self-Realization Meditation Healing Centre, Laurel Lane, Queen Camel, Yeovil, Somerset BA22 7NU. Tel: (01935) 850266. Fax: (01935) 850234. Under the guidance of Mata Yogananda, combining Raja and Kriya yogas.

Sivananda Yoga Vedanta Centre, 51 Felsham Road, London SWI5 1AZ. Tel: (0181) 780 0160. Fax: (0181) 780 0128.
E-mail: siva@dial.pipex.com. Courses, books, tapes, including meditation.

Skyros. Tel: (0171) 284 3065. Website: www.skyros.com/.Holidays in Greece and the Caribbean including meditation courses.

South London Buddhist Centre, 8 Trouville Road, Clapham, London SW4. Tel: (0181) 673 5570.

Sufi Order UK, Beauchamp Lodge, 2 Warwick Crescent, London W2 6NE.

Transcendental Meditation Association, Freepost, London SW1P 4YY. Tel: (0990) 143733. Write or phone for details of your nearest centre.

UK Council for Psychotherapy, 167–169 Great Portland Street, London W1N 5FB. Tel: (0171) 436 3002. Register of practitioners.

UK T'ai Chi Association, PO Box 159, Bromley, Kent BR1 3XX.
Tel: (0181) 289 5166. Send SAE for list of local teachers and information.

West London Buddhist Centre, 94 Westbourne Park Villas, London W2 5PL. Tel: (0171) 727 9382.

White Eagle, New Lands, Liss, Hampshire GU33 7HY. Meditation teachings.

The World Community for Christian Meditation, International Centre, 23 Kensington Square, London W8 5HN. Tel: (0171) 937 4679. Fax: (0171) 937 6790. E-mail: wccm@compuserve.com. Website: www.wccm.org.

Further Reading

Books on meditation
The Book of Meditation, Patricia Carrington (Element).
The Calm Technique, Paul Wilson (Thorsons, 1987).
Change Your Mind, Paramananda (Windhorse, 1996).
The Everyday Meditator, Osho (Boxtree, 1993).
Full Catastrophe Living: A practical guide to mindfulness, meditation and healing, Jon Kabat-Zinn (Delacorte Press, 1990).
How to Meditate, Lawrence LeShan (Thorsons, 1974).
Learn to Meditate Kit, Patricia Carrington (Element).
Meditation for Everybody, Louis Proto (Penguin, 1991).
Meditation, The First and Last Freedom, Osho (Rebel Books).
Moon Over Water, Jessica Macbeth (Gateway Books, 1990).
Peace of Mind – How you can learn to meditate and use the power of your mind, Ian Gawler (Prism Press, 1987).
Relaxation, Concentration and Meditation: Ancient skills for modern minds, Joel Levey (Wisdom Publications, 1987).
Teach Yourself Meditation, Naomi Feldman (Piatkus, 1990).
Teach Yourself to Meditate, Eric Harrison (Piatkus).
Teaching Meditation to Children, David Fontana and Ingrid Slack (Element, 1997).
The Three-Minute Meditator, Nina Feldman (Piatkus, 1990).

Other useful reading
Dr Dean Ornish's Program for Reversing Heart Disease, Dean Ornish (Random House, 1990).
Full Catastrophe Living: The relaxation and stress reduction program of the University of Massachusetts Medical Center, Jon Kabat-Zinn (Delacorte Press, 1990).
The Good Retreat Guide, Stafford Whiteaker (Rider, 1998). Guide to retreats in UK and parts of Europe.
The Handbook of Self-Healing: Your personal programme for better health and increased vitality, Meir Schneider and Maureen Larkin, with Dror Schneider (Penguin).

Molecules of Emotion: Why you feel the way you feel, Candace B. Pert (Simon & Schuster, 1998).

Peace, Love and Healing, Bernie Siegel (Harper & Row, 1989).

Rituals of Healing: Using imagery for health and wellness, J. Achterberg, B. Dossey and L. Kolkmeier (Bantam, 1994).

The Tao of Physics: An exploration of the parallels between modern physics and Eastern mysticism, Fritjof Capra (Bantam, 1984).

The Tibetan Book of Living and Dying, Sogyal Rinpoche (Rider).

Timeless Healing: The power and biology of belief, Herbert Benson (Scribner,1996).

Magazines

Caduceus, 38 Russell Terrace, Leamington Spa, Warwickshire CV31 1HE. Tel: (01926) 451897. Fax: (01926) 885565. E-mail: caduceus@oryx.demon.co.uk. Quarterly 'healing into wholeness'.

Kindred Spirit, Foxhole, Dartington, Totnes, Devon TQ9 6EB. Tel: (01803) 866686. Fax: (01803) 866591. Web: http://ww.kindredspirit.co.uk. Quarterly mind, body, spirit magazine.

Here's Health, Endeavour House, 189 Shaftesbury Avenue, London WC2H 8JG. Tel: (0171) 208 3209. Fax: (0171) 208 3583. Monthly.

Positive Health, 51 Queen Square, Bristol BSI 4LJ. Tel: (0117) 983 8851. Fax: (0117) 908 0097. Web: http://www. positivehealth. com. Bi-monthly.

Yoga Life, Sivananda Yoga Vedanta Centre, 51 Felsham Road, London SW15 1AZ. Tel: (0181) 780 0160. Fax: (0181) 780 0128. E-mail: siva@dial.pipex.com. Twice-yearly.

Index

active meditations, 75–84
affirmations, 55
ageing, meditation and, 20
Alexander technique, 97
alpha waves, 18, 19, 77, 83
anxiety, releasing, 17, 67, 96
aromatherapy, 90, 96
art meditations, 83–84
art therapy, 97
Atisha's meditation, 47–48
atmosphere, 37
attention, 12, 90
autogenics, 98

basic meditation, 22–31, 44, 83, 103
Beatles, 54
Benson, Herbert, 16, 58
beta waves, 19
Bible, 62
Blackmore, Dr Susan, 80
blood pressure, 16, 18
brain, 19, 62, 77
breath, 88
  attuning to, 14, 28, 51
  deep breathing, 65, 68, 88
  importance of, 22, 23
  meditating on, 12, 22–31, 44–48
  pattern of, 27
Buddha, 62
Buddhism, 11, 21, 44, 51, 52, 55, 80, 104, 105, 106

calm, 62
  cultivating, 68

candle-gazing, 51, 64, 65
chakras, 58–60
children, meditating with, 102
Christianity, 11, 55
  meditation and, 104, 105–106
circle dancing, 101
cleansing, 38
clear water visualisation, 96
clothing, 38
concentration, 13
connecting meditation, 69
Copenhagen University, 20
counselling, 90, 98
counting, 28
creativity, 83, 96, 97

dancing, 13, 75, 76–77
darkness meditation, 57–58, 83, 97
dhiker, 55
driving, 81

eating meditation, 82
energy, raising, 75, 76
Essenes, 57

fight-or-flight response, 18
flotation, 98
flower, meditating on, 64, 70
focus, 12, 26
Friends of the Western Buddhist Order, 106

gazing meditations 51–54, 64, 102
gibberish meditation, 62–63

golden light meditation, 73
guided visualisation, 90–97
   sample, 92–95
   understanding, 95
Gurdjieff, 70

Harrison, George, 11
hatha yoga, 87, 98
head rotations, 87
health, meditation and, 16–21
heart meditation, 45–47
Hinduism, 11, 54, 55, 104
holidays, 104, 105
humming, 56–57

International Journal of Nueorscience, 20
Islam, 55

Jesus prayer, 105

Kabat-Zinn, Jon, 32
Kabir, 76
Krishnamurti, 75
kundalini, 77–78

listening meditation, 65–67
lotus meditation, 75, 76
loving kindness meditation, 45–47

Maharishi Mahesh Yogi, 54
Main, John, 106
mandalas, 52
mantras, 54–56, 58, 105
massage, 90, 98
meditation, 11
   in everyday life, 80–83
   positions, 39
   programme, 34
   regular practice, 32–42
   retreats, 103–104

sample programmes, 34, 35
   space, 37
   times for, 36
Meher Baba, 51
metta bhavana, 44, 45–47
mindfulness meditation, 44
music, 65, 66–67, 77

nadabrahma, 57, 69
   for couples, 102
naming, 28
neuro linguistic programming, 55

om, 55
Ornish, Dean, 17
Osho, 22, 69, 77

painting meditations, 83
palming, 88
P'ang, 79
positive memories meditation, 72
progressive relaxation, 86–87
psychotherapy, 98

Quakers, 106

relaxation response, 16, 19
relaxing, 62, 72, 85, 86
   the eyes, 88
respiratory one method, 58
ritual, 41
Rumi, 90

self-gazing, 51–52
self-hypnosis, 98
shamanism, 98
sleep, 72
   assisting, 17, 71
   awareness meditation, 72
smoking meditation, 81
sound, 54
spirituality, 14, 16, 21, 99

stillness, 63, 73, 79, 89
stop meditation, 70
stress, 17
    releasing, 62, 63, 74, 85, 96
stretching, 87
Sufi, 55, 71
swimming, 80

t'ai chi, 90, 99
theta waves, 19
transcendental meditation (TM),
    18, 54

University of Massachusetts, 32
unravelling meditation, 71–72

vipassana meditation, 44–45

three methods, 44
    variations on, 45
visualisation, 90–96
    developing, 96

walking meditation, 45, 80
washing-up, 79, 80
whirling, 78–79
witnessing, 15, 29, 43, 77, 80
World Community for Christian
    Meditation, 106

yoga, 67, 76, 90, 99
Yogic teachings, 23

zazen, 44, 48–49, 50
Zen, 80, 104

ACHIEVING PERSONAL WELL-BEING
How to discover and balance your physical and emotional needs

James Chalmers

We tend to shut out natural daylight, work in soulless buildings, expose ourselves to pollution, and live on a diet of junk food. This highly original book is the result of a thorough investigation into how all these factors influence our physical and emotional welfare. It shows how daylight and the environment – including our astrological signs determine our personality and health, and how by understanding their effects we can take steps towards achieving physical and emotional well-being. The author explores the interrelation of body and mind, and reveals how only by balancing and managing their combined needs can we achieve personal well-being in all aspects of our lives. James Chalmers BSc CEng MIEE is a scientist and an artist. In this book he combines reason and imagination to offer you a remedy for the pressures of modern living.

144pp. illus. 1 85703 272 1.

UNLOCKING YOUR POTENTIAL
How to master your mind, life and destiny

Peter Marshall

Even the smartest individuals will not fulfil their potential on intellect alone; first they must free themselves from their own limiting expectations. If you really want to become master of your own life you will need to remove the barriers to success. This book will show you how to do it. It will introduce you to objective techniques for overcoming the limiting effects of the past: conditioning, misguided or obsolete teachings, repressed conflicts and the expectations imposed on us by others. Peter Marshall is a research psychologist, who specialises in mind and memory, and is a member of the Applied Psychology Research Group of the University of London. He is author of *How To Study and Learn* and *Research Methods* in this series.

144pp. 1 85703 252 7.

CONTROLLING ANXIETY
How to master fears and problems and start living with confidence

William Stewart

Many people suffer from differing degrees of anxiety. Mild anxiety is a feeling common to us all – an unavoidable part of human personality. Severe anxiety on the other hand can control our lives The aim of this hook is to provide a knowledge base for sufferers and others, and to suggest strategies that will help people manage their anxiety and regain control of their lives. It is also a valuable handbook for those who work in healthcare and counselling. William Stewart is a freelance counsellor, supervisor and author. His background is in nursing, psychiatric social work, and student counselling and lecturing at a London college of nursing. He is author of *Building Self-Esteem* and co-author of *Learning to Counsel* in this series.

144pp. illus. 1 85703 267 5.

THRIVING ON STRESS
How to manage pressures and transform your life

Jan Sutton

The pressures of modern life make us susceptible to stress. However not all stress is negative – if managed effectively we can positively thrive on it. Peak performance stress stimulates activity, enhances creativity, and motivates us to live happy and fulfilling lives. Drawing on her experience as a counsellor, stress management and assertiveness trainer, Jan Sutton not only equips you with easily mastered strategies for conquering negative stress, she also offers you a personal development programme for building self-esteem and self-confidence. The book is complete with comprehensive case studies, illustrations, and practical activities. Jan Sutton (Dip CPC) is co-author (with William Stewart) of *Learning to Counsel* in this series.

192pp. illus. 1 8703 238 1.